DOG

THE ~~ ꜱ-EYE
VIEW ~~ ON TACKLING
PET PROBLEMS

DILEMMAS

DOG DILEMMAS

THE DOG'S-EYE VIEW ON TACKLING PET PROBLEMS

SOPHIE COLLINS

AMMONITE
PRESS

First published 2019 by
Ammonite Press
an imprint of Guild of Master Craftsman Publications Ltd
Castle Place, 166 High Street, Lewes,
East Sussex, BN7 1XU
United Kingdom
www.ammonitepress.com

ISBN 978 1 78145 336 0

Publisher: Jason Hook
Design Manager: Robin Shields
Editor: Jamie Pumfrey
Photographer: Neil Grundy
Designer: Wayne Blades
Retouching and Cutouts: Jon Hoag and Alex Bailey

Colour reproduction by GMC Reprographics
Printed and bound in China

CONTENTS

Introduction 6
The cast 8

CHAPTER ONE 10
Whose problem is it, anyway?

What dogs do naturally 12
What dogs don't do naturally 16
Getting to know your dog 20
Managing expectations 24
Speaking 'dog' 28
Changing attitudes 34

CHAPTER TWO 38
Dilemmas at home

My dog is finding it hard to settle 40
How to help your dog to settle 42
My dog is difficult to house-train 44
How to start a house-training programme 46
My dog charges at the door 50
How to teach the door sequence 52
My dog's unsure of strangers 54
How to tackle your dog's fears 56
My dog is possessive 58
How to learn to swap 60
I can't find a food to suit my dog 62
How to find a diet that will work 64
My dog goes from 0-60 in a nanosecond 66
How to introduce pause time 68

CHAPTER THREE 70
Out and about

My dog pulls and weaves on the lead 72
How to make your dog love the lead 74
My dog won't come when I call 76
How to get my dog to come back 78
My dog's scared of road noise 82
How to hear noise without fear 84
My dog doesn't play well with others 86
How to spot and stop a pushy player 88
How to learn to relax around other dogs 90
My dog doesn't want to go for a walk 92
How to break the no-walk habit 94

CHAPTER FOUR 96
Working with worries

Learning by problem solving 98
How to stop a toy fixation 100
How to deal with a ball junkie 102
Learning to cope with being home alone 104
How to deal with grief 106
Taking back control of the furniture 108
How to prevent nipping 110
How to have a dog-free dinner time 112
How to make friends with the postal worker 114
Should we try crate training? 116
How to distract from humping 118
Taking the stress out of meeting new people 120
When to get professional help 122

Further reading 124
Index 126
Acknowledgments 128

INTRODUCTION

Dogs live in our world, not the other way around, but they're mostly so good at the life-share – at working with our structures and fitting in with our rules – that this is easily forgotten. The dog/human relationship is thought to have begun anything up to 30,000 years ago, and it remains unique: no other two species have such a close connection.

The dog's place in a human household has changed radically from a century or two ago. In the past, most dogs worked. Today, while there are still plenty of dogs with clearly defined jobs to do, the vast majority live as companions to their humans – they're 'just' pets. And while a working dog's life may seem complicated, whether his career consists of herding sheep or sniffing out drugs, the companion dog's role is, if anything, even more demanding. He needs to pick up the rules of a human household and to live within them, usually without the intensive training given to the working dog.

If you think that sounds simple, try to imagine how you, a human, would cope if you had to swap the society and rules of your own species for those of a different one: how you would manage if, say, you were transplanted into the company of a herd of elephants. Or a pride of lions? Even though dogs have had thousands of years of practice, we still ask a lot of them.

The boundaries for companion dogs have become much more flexible, too. Few dogs are expected to sleep in an outside kennel any more, and most pets are given food tailored to their needs rather than being fed scraps. So far, so good – no dog ever complained about having too comfortable a bed, overly digestible food, or too many toys. But the downside to an easier life is that our expectations around canine behaviour have risen sky-high.

▼ **The importance of teaching**
Dogs are often expected to know what we want of them when we haven't taken enough trouble to teach them and make sure that they understand what we mean.

CITIZEN DOG

The good news is that most dogs are naturally upstanding citizens, quick on the uptake and eager to fit in, and as a result problems arise far less often than you might expect. But when they do – when your dog nips unexpectedly, or gets guardy over a valued toy, or refuses to come back when you call him in the park – it helps to try to understand the situation the way he sees it, and sort out a solution that's workable for both of you.

Far more is known today about what it is like to be a dog – from being a rare subject for scholarly research just 20 years ago, dogs have become recent star-players in cognition and behavioural studies. In the past they were considered uninteresting subjects precisely because of the closeness of their relationship with humans, but in the last two decades attitudes have changed and now dogs have become interesting precisely because of the way in which they successfully live alongside us. As a result, far more has been discovered about both how and why dogs behave in certain ways. This book shows how we can use this knowlege to build a new relationship with our pets, and to solve the dog dilemmas that can be so frustrating to dog and owner alike.

▲ Knowledge is power
While there's still an awful lot that we don't know, having more scientific insight has been invaluable in updating our attitudes to our pets.

DOG'S-EYE VIEW

HOW IT WORKS

Throughout this book you'll find 'Dog's-eye view' boxes. These take into account the way in which I, your dog, may see things. They will help to demonstrate that there are always at least two sides to any situation: mine and yours! After all, the easiest way to persuade others to come around to your way of seeing things is to recognize the way they see things themselves. And that goes for me, too!

Note: There's a tradition of referring to the dog as 'he' in dog books, and we've stuck with it for reasons of clarity – except when the subject of the text is specifically female.

THE CAST...

ROO

SNOOP

EDISON

SNOOPY

BEAR

PHOEBE

CLARENCE

AGATHA

FREDDIE

DIZZY

FRANKIE

RUBY

OZZY

HENRY

SMUDGE

HUNNY

BUDDY

LUNA

CHAPTER ONE

WHOSE PROBLEM IS IT, **ANYWAY?**

Before you jump in and try to resolve any problems or dilemmas you're having with your dog, it helps to know something about what makes him tick. This chapter fills in some of the background to our relationship with dogs – it looks at the behaviours that come naturally to most dogs (plus some of the behaviours that don't); at what recent research has taught us about what it's like to be a dog; and, finally, at our ideas about how a dog should behave, and how realistic – or necessary – those are to achieve. And because there are two species in the canine/human relationship, we take an additional look at how humans work in relation to dogs.

WHAT DOGS DO
NATURALLY

Have you ever wondered what it's actually like to be a dog? Try to imagine a world in which your senses have been rearranged, so that you start to get a sense of how our canine friends actually see, hear, smell and feel. It will start to give you an insight into why they behave in the way that they do.

LISTENING

Your hearing has become much keener; you can hear things that were previously off the scale to human ears and some noises seem unbearably loud or sharp – to the point where you're stimulated to join in with your own (barking, howling) contribution. What's more, you can use the muscles at the base of your ear to turn it, like an ear trumpet, to catch the maximum amount of any specific noise (and even when you have heavy, drop ears, rather than the upright kind, the interior mechanism is the same).

▶ **How does a dog hear?**
The mechanics of canine hearing are directional: dogs have muscles at the base that will swivel the ear in the direction of interesting sounds to hear them better.

SMELLING

The biggest difference of all, though, is the change in your sense of smell. It's so sensitive that it's far and away the sense you rely on the most: what you can smell tells you much more about your surroundings than what you can see, and you can identify single strands of odour in the same way that an art expert would be able to distinguish individual brushstrokes in the painting of an Old Master.

DOG'S-EYE VIEW

WHY I SNIFF

Sniffing is one of the most fascinating things I can do – much as you may not be able to take your eyes off a startling sight, so I find it hard to take my nose away from a particularly complex or intriguing smell. Taking me to places where I'm guaranteed to find rich, new smells – a walk in the country or a day at the beach for a city dog, say – feels as exciting as I imagine a trip to the theatre or a major art show would be for a person.

▲ **Why the urge to sniff?**
Once you know how turbo-powered his sense of smell is, a dog's overwhelming impulse to sniff (and to mark) becomes much more understandable. Smelling surely amounts to reading the news in dog terms: both on the street and out in the countryside, it tells you what's going on, and who's been around and when.

SCENT RECEPTORS

When it comes to scenting ability, not all dogs are created equal. Top of the canine scent tree comes the bloodhound with an estimated 300 million scent receptors. Beagles score around average with about 225 million receptors – but if you assumed that flat-nosed dogs wouldn't be able to scent as effectively, you'd be wrong: in a smell-off in 2015, performed under scientific conditions, pugs (with an estimated 200 million receptors), surprisingly, outperformed German shepherds.

200,000,000

Pug

225,000,000

Beagle

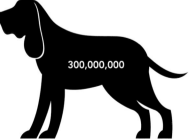

300,000,000

Bloodhound

LOOKING

Although it's still important to you, sight no longer dominates. You can't see a very broad spectrum of colours and you have trouble distinguishing between red and green, but you have broader 'windscreen' vision – not quite eyes in the back of your head, but certainly eyes that go round the sides more than you're used to.

You can see movement better, too – while you don't notice the finer detail of things when they're still, you can catch the tiniest motion anywhere in your field of vision (good for chasing down a squirrel when there happens to be one nearby).

BREAK DOWN ROUTINES

One of the ways that behaviourists recommend dealing with a dog suffering from stress and anxiety is to behave in a way that confuses his observations. For example, one suggestion to help him cope with separation anxiety is for his owner to consciously break down routines so that the dog can no longer predict when he's going to be left, and therefore doesn't have the chance to rev up his anxiety about it in advance.

▲ High alert

Dogs are top-level observers, generally far better than even the most observant human. Most have every aspect of their – and your – daily routine down, to the tiniest detail, particularly when they've learned from experience the parts of it that usually relate to them. Your dog will know all the signs that show you're going out, and he'll also be familiar with which ones show whether or not he's coming too.

► Do dogs feel lonely?

Generally dogs aren't good at being alone: it isn't natural for them, which is why you should accustom puppies to spending time alone gradually and gently. The jury is out on the number of emotions we share with dogs, but everyone agrees that even quite self-sufficient dogs experience loneliness if they're on their own for prolonged periods of time.

INSTINCT

Sense-wise you may be very different to humans, but there's a key thing you both share as species: you're social animals, and you're impressively adaptable in all sorts of group situations.

If you've been adequately socialized as a puppy, you will behave fluently and confidently around other dogs and people. There is no way of knowing whether you consciously recognize the differences between species or whether other dogs are better at understanding your communication systems than people are, but one thing is certain: you never stop communicating, and your body language is highly expressive.

◄ How does he know when it's suppertime?

Owners often observe how accurate dogs' internal clocks seem to be when it comes to mealtimes, but it's just as likely that dogs use their powers of observation to become familiar with all the things you do before they get their dinner and are conducting an internal countdown.

WHAT DOGS DON'T
DO NATURALLY

Unless they are trained, dogs don't know what you want them to do – nor do they understand much of what we say when we talk. This sounds obvious, but to a dog a number of the things that you are keen to teach them aren't natural behaviours for them. So they don't even have a head start on what it is you might want them to do. And unless they're taught very precisely to connect such behaviour with a verbal cue, talking them through it won't work either.

WALKING ON A LEAD
People are used to the idea of walking side-by-side (often, in dog terms, very slowly indeed). But to a dog, it's unnatural behaviour: dogs don't stroll alongside one another, even when they want to get to the same place. Watch some canine friends off-lead – you'll see them circle, break off to pursue a smell, charge ahead and fall behind. And this is probably why teaching a dog to walk to heel can take a while, even with a cooperative dog who loves the treats you've got on offer.

▼ How does a lead feel?
It is no surprise it takes dogs a long time to feel comfortable walking to heel. You're not just asking them to do something in a certain way, you're asking them to grasp an altogether unfamiliar concept.

TOUCHING: HUMAN VS DOG

Walking to heel isn't the only thing that doesn't come naturally. Dogs get used to being handled tactlessly – in canine terms, that is – because so very many humans do it. Humans hug (so do chimpanzees – a reminder that we're essentially apes), but dogs don't, yet millions of dogs submit every day to being hugged because it makes their human feel good.

◄ How does it feel to be hugged?
Look at the face of a dog being hugged and it rarely looks truly relaxed, even if the dog is happy to tolerate it.

▼ Let him come to you
You probably remember the uncomfortable feeling of being forced to meet new people when you were a shy kid; it was always better when you were left to say hello in your own time. The same holds for some dogs; while some love everyone instantly, others like to take their time meeting someone new.

DOG'S-EYE VIEW

WHY I LET YOU HUG ME

To me, an arm around my shoulder feels the same way as when another dog puts his paw over me, and he isn't playing – a bit threatening. Since you're familiar and I like you, I put up with it, and sometimes I'll lick your face, which is a habit I learned as a puppy when I wanted to appease a grown dog; it makes the whole situation feel more relaxed to me.

INTERACTING WITH CHILDREN

While remembering what comes naturally to dogs is always helpful, there's one area of life in which it's crucial, and that's when a dog spends any time around children, particularly the under-fives. Any interaction between dogs and children should always be supervised, and you can avoid trouble by teaching dogs and children together, so that the dog isn't the subject of unwelcome attention from the child, and the child doesn't become the subject of fear or defensiveness for the dog.

It's usually fairly obvious whether or not a dog loves children. But even if he does, there are things about children that may disconcert or frighten him:

- Children may not yet have the consistency or control to handle a dog gently and appropriately.
- Their noises tend to be high-pitched, irregular and loud.
- If you have a dog that's interested in hunting (and it's never safe to assume that any dog isn't), a toddler squealing may trigger his arousal levels into 'hunt' mode.
- A small child may eyeball a dog in what will look like confrontation to him – and toddlers are often at face level to a dog.

▼ Dogs and children

There are a number of reasons to be extremely careful about managing the interactions between small children and dogs, whether or not they are familiar with one another. Even dogs you may have considered bomb-proof can't always cope with every aspect of small children.

WHY BITES HAPPEN

Biting is a last resort for a dog. Usually he will have tried to back out of an uncomfortable situation and will have given a warning (growls have a purpose). Only after these have failed will he bite. Given how much dog/human contact there is, the incidence of dogs biting people is very low indeed. However, a disproportionate number of bites are to children, and it's not fair to either the child or the dog to allow a situation to arise where there's any chance of a bite. The reason to raise the whole subject of 'dog-bites-child' is not because it is common, but because it's so awful when it does happen.

MAKE RULES FOR CHILDREN

Children should be taught some basic safety rules for engaging respectfully with dogs.

- Leave a dog alone when he's eating his meals or resting
- Don't wake a sleeping dog suddenly by touching him or making a loud noise near him
- Be aware that high-pitched shouting or screaming, particularly when you're running around, may upset the dog – he may feel that there's a problem that he needs to sort out (by joining in and jumping around barking himself)
- If it looks as though noise and rushing about are upsetting the dog, calm down, be still, and lower your voices.

▲ Keeping things positive
Although even young children should be taught basic safety rules around dogs, turn the picture more positive by involving them in 'training' the family dog. Giving treats in return for sits, holding out a hand to be sniffed (rather than imposing touch on the dog), or throwing a ball for games of fetch can all be built into daily family activities. This should help ensure that dogs and kids are comfortable around each other.

19

GETTING TO KNOW
YOUR DOG

Dog owners – or most of them – know better than to generalize. Dogs have personalities, just as people do: they have plenty in common with the rest of their species, but not everything. In the same way that you can't say 'People like sport', you can't say 'Dogs enjoy playing fetch'. Some, probably even most, do; some don't.

YOUR DOG'S PERSONALITY

Your dog's best chance of being thoroughly understood lies with you, his owner. And dogs show as much variety in personality and individual preference as people do. Sometimes, though, preconceptions of how they typically are, or how a certain breed 'ought' to be – or even, in the case of your own dog, what you'd like him to be – get in the way of seeing the dog in front of you.

▼ **What is your dog's play style?**
Your dog may not always play as you'd expect; try out different toys and games to find out which has the strongest appeal to him. Tug, fetch, frisbee, hunt-the-treat: there are plenty of ways to play.

WATCH YOUR DOG PLAY

Take time to carefully watch your dog at play and ask yourself the following questions:

- Who does he pick to play with, and does he spend most of the time chasing, or does he like wrestling?
- Does he get madly excited playing? So much so that you sometimes have to engineer a break to calm things down?
- Does he like to break up play between other dogs, or is he so engaged in his own affairs that he doesn't pay much attention to what a larger group is doing around him?
- How does he instigate a game – does he hang around on the margins, waiting for an invitation, or does he go straight in, confidently identifying a playmate?

Use the information you collect to understand who your dog really is. He may be shyer or more gregarious than you'd assumed.

DOGWATCHING

The best way to get to know your dog better is to watch him at odd moments, when he's mixing with other dogs, socializing with people he knows and is comfortable with, and meeting new people and dogs. Spend a few minutes observing him, too, when there's nothing particular going on – downtime can tell you as much as when he's up and active. What will you learn? Possibly nothing hugely new – but it will help you consolidate the knowledge that you have.

You don't necessarily have to use the knowledge immediately: dogwatching is a spectator sport – but the more familiar you are with the way your dog behaves in a whole range of different situations, the easier it will be to deal confidently with problems and dilemmas when they arise – and, sometimes, to head off trouble before it even happens.

▲ Game or trick?
Smart dogs sometimes enjoy trick training as much as 'straight' play. It means more time with you, with plenty of encouragement and treats, too. If you want to broaden his repertoire, try teaching your dog something – to shake hands, perhaps, or stand up on his hind legs when asked.

DO YOU KNOW YOUR DOG?

A better all-round knowledge of your dog will also give you an idea of areas in which he would be helped by your support. You'll only get ideas for what your dog might need by discovering as much as you can about who he is, and what his likes and dislikes are – they may not be what you've always assumed.

A dog who is very competitive in play, for example, might, when it comes to playing with you, benefit more from running, fetching and swapping toys than from playing tug. However enjoyable this may be for him, it may ramp up his competitive side.

DOES YOUR DOG KNOW YOU?

We're aware that our dog knows what we do. But how conscious is he of the differences between you? Does he know on some

▲ Play or competition?

Competitive games are just as common for canines as humans. But unevenly matched dogs have been noted to hold back a little when playing with a weaker partner. Winning doesn't always seem to be the point: the pleasure comes out of the game itself.

▼ What if your dog doesn't want to play?

Not every dog likes playing: some seem more serious minded, a few apparently can't see the point of toys. Remember that play isn't compulsory: if you can rule out illness, he's getting plenty of exercise, and he doesn't seem bored, leave him be.

level, for example, that you are a different species from him? Or does he think of you as some kind of very slow dog with almost no sense of smell?

Current science says that your dog does know you're different. He knows that you are 'management' in his life and that resources are controlled by you, and he knows that you're alive (dogs respond quite differently to objects that move that aren't alive). But both of these may come under some vague cognitive umbrella that doesn't question, but broadly just accepts the status quo. Cognition studies are, however, continuing to reveal more and more about dogs' awareness and sense of self.

MANAGING
EXPECTATIONS

You may have seen it; it's one of the best dog cartoons there is, and it pops up everywhere from Facebook to greetings cards. In the first frame, a drowning man is calling back to his smart-looking dog on the shore: 'Lassie, get help!' In the second frame, the same dog is seen lying back on an analyst's couch, gesturing with an eloquent paw, while the earnest doctor takes notes. It's funny because it skews human expectations of dogs. Lassie doesn't run for help; instead, she misunderstands her human, but in the most sophisticated way: she goes to her appointment with her analyst. And of course, real dogs don't have analysts – which in a way is a pity because, sometimes, human expectations must drive them mad.

WHAT'S THAT YOU SAY?

As humans we are used to communicating with speech, first and foremost, and we often can't stop even when, objectively, we know that our dogs don't understand. Studies of human communication show that speech comes naturally to us: faced with someone (or some dog) who doesn't appear to understand what we're saying, we say it again, but this time with a slightly raised voice.

Owners often claim that dogs understand a lot of what they say. However, studies of communication in dogs seem to show that, while dogs are excellent at reading human body language and have great memories for the contexts in which things have happened in the past (and may therefore happen again), even the smartest dog doesn't seem to have a very sophisticated understanding of the meanings of different words. It's doubtful whether any dog could distinguish accurately between verbs and nouns, much less adjectives. Why not? Since dogs don't talk, interpreting speech may not come very high up the agenda for them. They're certainly fast at interpreting, and reacting to, tone of voice (see the Why I Look Guilty box on page 27). This may matter more, as it will help them anticipate the consequences of what's being said.

Lassie, even if highly trained, is unlikely to bark an explanation of what's happening to a potential helper – much less keep her appointment with the analyst.

HOW BIG IS YOUR DOG'S VOCABULARY?

BASIC
Popular science holds that most pet dogs understand 50 words.

AVERAGE
Dog expert Stanley Coren, on the other hand, thinks the 'average' dog knows around 165 words.

GENIUS?
Record-breaking collie Chaser was found to recognize more than a thousand objects by name. All nouns, though – it wasn't clear whether he could tell the difference between 'being' words (nouns) and 'doing' words (verbs).

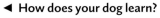

◀ How does your dog learn?

Dogs are great at putting the clues together. And most learn quickly from experience. If the mention of a walk is always followed by, well, a walk, they'll be fast to pick up on it. But most dogs don't seem to be able to distinguish different categories of word.

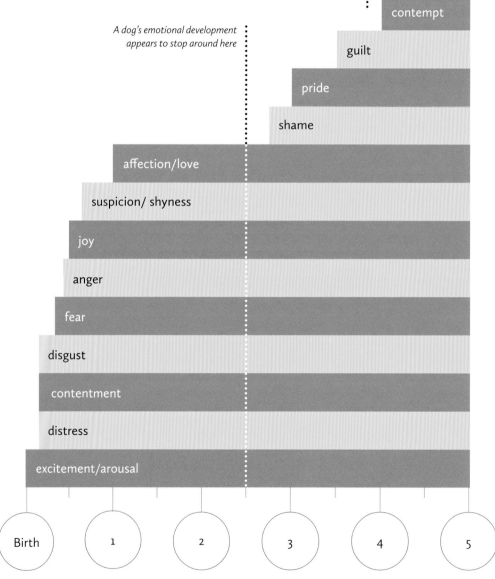

WHAT DOES MY DOG FEEL?

We know dogs have feelings, but which feelings and to what range? Most cognition experts believe that an adult dog has around the same emotional range as a two-year-old human. What this means is that he can feel pleasure, affection, excitement, fear, worry and anger, but that some of the more nuanced feelings such as contempt, guilt and shame aren't in his repertoire.

contempt

A dog's emotional development appears to stop around here

guilt

pride

shame

affection/love

suspicion/ shyness

joy

anger

fear

disgust

contentment

distress

excitement/arousal

Birth   1   2   3   4   5

Age at which human emotions appear (years)

DO DOGS LOVE THEIR OWNERS?

Almost all owners want to believe not only that dogs can feel love, but that their dogs love them. And going by the scientific as well as the emotional evidence, they're probably right. Dogs generally seem to like the company of their owners best.

Not only that, but in scent trials when dogs were offered a range of smells including those of both familiar and unfamiliar dogs and people, the caudate nucleus, the area of the brain associated with enjoyment, not only lit up when they came to their owners' scent, but lit up more strongly than in any other case, including the scents of dogs that were their friends and that they regularly played with. The touch of their owners also increased dogs' oxytocin levels – and oxytocin is the hormone most closely associated, in humans, with tactile affection and, yes, love.

CAN MY DOG FEEL EMPATHY?

One of the reasons humans enjoy dogs' company so much is that dogs seem to us to live in the moment, without concern for what's to come or what has gone before. As a result, we find it easier to dismiss our own worries in dogs' company. But most people also discover empathy in their dogs. There's as yet no way of measuring canine empathy, but we do know that dogs react to different expressions on the faces of people as well as those of other dogs. So it may be that they can take it one step further and read – and show empathy for – our moods. We visit a lot of expectations on them, but the idea that they know how we feel may be realistic.

▼ As happy as he looks?
To a human eye, this little terrier looks straightforwardly happy – but how many other feelings are within his range?

DOG'S-EYE VIEW

WHY I LOOK GUILTY

I can tell you when I'm happy and when I'm worried with my ears, tail and general demeanour. But you still sometimes misread me – when you shouted the other day, I tucked my tail and lowered my head because I hate you being angry with me. I don't understand what the word 'guilty' actually means. The peeing in the kitchen while you were out? To be honest, I'd long since forgotten about that.

27

SPEAKING
'DOG'

When dog owners consult the professionals because their pet has behaved in an unexpected – problematic – way, behaviourists and trainers are very used to hearing them say that 'it just came out of nowhere'. 'One moment he seemed quite happy, wagging his tail, and then he suddenly growled', for example. But dog behaviour hardly ever comes out of nowhere, and if you learn how to look, and to take context into account too, there are nearly always signs of how a dog is feeling. Given that he can't speak, these signs come in the form of his body language.

BODY LANGUAGE

While sometimes your dog's body language may be self-evident, at other times it's subtle and takes a bit of practice to decipher. If you get into the habit of watching both your dog and others, though, before long you'll notice patterns in their body language, both when they're interacting and when they're with their humans. Of course, your dog is far more than a collection of body parts. But just as you can see what people's expressions tell you, so you can add up what the different parts of a dog's body are telling you to get a good idea of how he feels. Waggy and happy? Tense and still? Slow and a bit apprehensive? And when a problem does arise, whether it's a play session that's getting too intense or one dog bullying another, you'll be able to spot it and deal with it early on.

DELIBERATE OR NOT?

Just as with people, the body signs dogs send may be deliberate communication – for example, the classic 'play bow' (the front-paws-flat, rear-in-air, tail-held-high pose, that a dog will use to invite another dog to play) is entirely aimed at another dog, or sometimes a favoured person.

However, signs such as a shy dog with his tail tucked under, head down, or trying to make himself look smaller, are more likely to be involuntary.

▼ Classic play bow

A dog in this posture is sending a message universally understood between dogs. Bottom in air; forepaws flat on the floor; relaxed, open mouth and happy, squinty eyes are all inviting someone else to play.

HOW TO READ EYES

At one end of the spectrum, a happy dog's eyes may look a little 'squinty'; the muscles in the corners are loose and relaxed. At the other, dogs may show 'hard eye': narrowed eyes with the muscles around them held tight. Hard eyes combined with a very still body posture tend to spell trouble. Dramatically widened eyes, to the point at which the whites show, indicate a fearful dog.

In ordinary meet-and-greets, dogs don't tend to look each other directly in the eye; it's too likely to be seen as challenging. And in situations where two dogs are in uncomfortably close proximity, you will often see them deliberately looking away from one another, apparently to avoid any confrontational interpretation.

▲ Happy
Look at a relaxed dog and you'll nearly always see a slightly 'squinty' eye. Hard to describe, but easy to recognize once spotted, it signifies a happy, laid-back mood.

▲ Focused
Less relaxed – the eyes lose their squinty look – but there's no muscle tension at the corners. This dog is concentrating on something specific.

▲ Animated
Face forwards, and if you look closely you can see that his eyes have moved forwards, too. This is the engaged face of a dog that's about to get involved.

▲ Unsure
Ears at half-mast and slightly back like this show a dog who's feeling a degree of uncertainty about his surroundings.

▲ Alert
Ears fully up and pointing forwards signify an alert dog who's fully engaged with whatever is around him.

▲ Relaxed
Fully down, this is the relaxed ear of a dog who's in neutral: just minding his own business, without anything very distracting going on.

HOW TO READ EARS

Understanding a dog's ear movements depends a good deal on his breed. The muscles at the base of the ear will always be doing the same thing, whatever type of dog you're looking at, but it's much easier for you to see what's going on if you're looking at a German shepherd than a pug or a bloodhound.

Ears generally signal how much attention a dog is paying. Pricked up and alert, he's showing interest, and the more 'alert' the ears, the more engaged the dog. This doesn't tell you anything about the type of interest, only its degree.

Ears held hard back indicate a degree of discomfort; again, the all-round body language will give you more clues on how, or even whether, the dog is going to act on it.

HOW TO READ A MOUTH

It's the corners of a dog's mouth – the commissures – that tell you the most. As with his eyes, relaxed muscles at the mouth corners indicate a relaxed dog, while tight muscles at the corners are a sign of tension, and may be a prelude to his lips curling back.

Don't mix this up with play-fighting: dogs will mimic tight-mouth snarling and so on when playing with one another (we've all seen pairs of dogs in apparently very snarly, bitey play), but it's intercut with wavy tails and relaxed, loose body language.

▲ **Happy**
Open mouth without any tension in the corner muscles, combined with a relaxed, slightly lolling tongue are signs of a relaxed, happy dog.

▲ **Anxious**
A down, tucked tail like this tends to show a degree of anxiety; if it's tightly tucked under, the dog may be fearful.

▲ **Relaxed**
Held at half-mast but loosely, this tail is in neutral.

▲ **Eager**
Up but not yet over – this is an active, interested tail. If you could see the other end of this terrier, he'd likely be headed forwards, ready to engage.

▲ Uncertain
Mid-tongue flick. Dogs tend to use tongue flicks as a sign of uncertainty – they'll use one when they're passing another dog they're not quite sure of, for instance.

▲ Neutral
A shut mouth shows less relaxation than an open one, but there's no tightness in the corners here, so the mood indicates neutrality rather than defensiveness.

▲ Curly
The curly tail is the hard-to-read joker in the pack: it doesn't often uncurl to let you know what's going on. With a curly-tailed dog, take a look at his ears, eyes and mouth for other indicators.

HOW TO READ A TAIL

Now that docked tails have become much rarer – it's illegal in many countries to dock the tail of any but a working dog – it's easier to see just how expressive almost all dogs' tails are. The higher the tail, the more alert/confident the dog, while tails carried very low, or in extreme cases tucked between the back legs, signify apprehension or even fear. A dog simply going about his business often carries his tail near-horizontally – loose, wavy and relaxed.

Don't always read a moving tail as a 'wag': a tail held high and stiff but moving slowly from side to side is not a friendly sign, but an indicator of an increasingly tense dog. Some research has shown that even the direction of the wag has a significance: dogs wag to the right when they're happy/receptive, and to the left when they're less confident/would prefer to back off from a situation.

33

CHANGING
ATTITUDES

Up until fairly recently, the domestic dog wasn't considered to be a worthy subject for serious research. Dogs were thought to be too familiar and too much affected by their close relationship with humans to be interesting from a scientific point of view. That changed in the 1990s, and now pet dogs are favourites in the research labs. As a result, a broader picture of the lives of dogs and of their abilities has filtered down to a much wider audience. Some misconceptions have been dispelled, too, and even some of the everyday language used about dogs has fallen out of fashion as it was found to be inaccurate or misleading.

PACK ANIMALS? NOT REALLY

It used to be a favourite phrase to say that dogs were 'pack' animals, in the same way that wolves are. DNA-wise, wolves are identical to dogs – to the degree that the two can interbreed – but they are still different species, and the more dogs that were studied, the less like wolves they seemed.

Dogs are social animals, but there are few if any indications that they perceive either fellow dogs or humans in the same household as comprising their 'pack' in the feral sense the word implies. Instead, dogs seem to be instinctively adept at picking up social signals, and flexibly cooperating within the status quo. And since they are outstanding observers of the behaviour of both their own and other species, their unique ability to integrate with human groups becomes more explicable: they understand how to fit in. Their 'watch and learn' way of operating even led to a whole series of experiments in which pet dogs performed quite elaborate sequences of actions simply by following humans doing them.

▼ **Working together**
The majority of dogs cooperate sensibly together in an all-round beneficial situation. Here, faced with a treat handout, both dogs focus on the treat-giver rather than entering into competition with one another.

IS A DOG JUST A WOLF IN A HOUSE?

Dogs aren't nearly as wolf-like as it used to be believed (actually, in terms of savagery and bloodthirsty behaviour, wolves aren't as wolf-like as people used to think, either). Both species understand the value of cooperation, but while wolves limit this to their own species and pack, dogs have developed a strong, useful cooperation with a completely different species – humans.

- Wild
- Cooperates well with its own species, working in a pack
- Lives independently, with its own role within the pack
- Hunts and scavenges for food (incidentally, wolves are very conservative eaters)
- Plays only as a cub

- Domesticated
- Cooperates well both with its own species and with humans
- Lives dependently, but relies on its humans to play the 'leader' role
- Relies on food being supplied, and eats widely and opportunistically (sometimes, where the opportunity arises, with supplemental hunting)
- Continues to play in adulthood

DOMINANCE THEORY DEBUNKED

More research also dismissed a longstanding theory that had largely developed out of the wolf-in-the-house image of the dog. For a long time it was believed that owners had to be 'pack leaders', showing their dogs who was boss. Dogs need to know that they are not in charge, the theory went, or they will try to attain dominance over their owners, which can lead to all kinds of unhappy outcomes at home.

For many years this led to training methods that were punishment-based, unsympathetic at best and near-abusive at worst. Over time, though, it became apparent that punishing dogs for behaving in unwanted ways did not actually work. The short-term result might be that the behaviour stopped (after all, if someone shouts at you or physically hurts you for doing something, you tend to stop doing it); but, in the longer term, dogs became afraid of their owners and resorted to fear-based aggression which made the initial problems a hundred times worse.

▲ **Winner takes all**
'Dominance' is a term used to express who wins the resources – in this case, a bowl of food. Often all you will see in a negotiation over which canine wins out is a calm certainty on the part of the 'dominant' party.

DOG'S-EYE VIEW

WHO'S RUNNING THINGS?

I prefer to be clear about who's in charge, but that doesn't mean that there shouldn't be give-and-take in our relationship. I'm only too happy to play follow-my-leader so long as my human has got the sense to inspire confidence and to understand that, when I play up, it's because I need reassurance. Punishment is a mug's game: it simply makes me apprehensive and snappy.

POSITIVITY, NOT DOMINANCE

In the study of dogs, 'dominance' has never referred to an inherent characteristic of a dog, but rather to situations in which the division of resources – access to food, perhaps, or to attention from an owner – is decided. People who own more than one dog often notice that which dog gets what is usually agreed between them without any outward display of force or aggression; out of two dogs, the one who gets the prime sleeping spot in front of the fire may be described as 'dominant' because he gained that asset; but, in another situation, the second dog may be the first to claim and retain a chew toy – in which case, he is the 'dominant' one. Dominance is an aspect of a situation, and a description of a behaviour, rather than a characteristic of the dog, but was twisted for a while to fit a theory that, scientifically, has now been comprehensively debunked.

Dominance theory, in the form of 'needing to show the dog who's boss', still lingers on, though, and it's worth describing what it is and how it came about purely so that it can be avoided. Positive, non-confrontational training methods are winning out; and, from a dog's point of view, positive training enables him to learn without fear and to develop a deeper bond with his owner. From the owner's viewpoint, too, the better you understand a dog, the better the relationship between you will be.

▶ **Dealing with uncertainty**
Kindly reassurance is key with a dog that lacks confidence; any kind of confrontation will only set him back and teach him to be fearful.

CHANGING ATTITUDES

CHAPTER TWO

DILEMMAS
AT HOME

This chapter looks at dilemmas that arise in and around the house. Whether

you're trying to settle in a new dog, reinforce shaky house-training or instil some

manners around the exciting territory of the front door, you'll find a range of

easily implemented strategies to try, never forgetting how the situation may

look from your dog's point of view. All of them will reinforce your role as the

person your dog looks to when he needs help in making sense of the world and

understanding the rules to live by.

MY DOG IS FINDING IT
HARD TO SETTLE

When it comes to getting a new dog, more and more people are looking to rescue centres, and one obvious consequence is that more people are bringing home an adult dog. New owners may imagine that the settling-in process will be faster and easier than it would be with a puppy. But just as a puppy would – often even more so – an adult dog needs time to settle. Breeders and rescuers agree that making any judgement of a new dog's behaviour or personality over the first few days, much less the first few hours, is pointless. You need to give him time to settle in.

Dog trainers and behaviourists are used to taking calls from new owners who have arrived home with their dog just a few days – or even hours – earlier. They ask for help because:

- his behaviour is challenging
- he paces and won't settle down
- he keeps barking
- he doesn't appear to be house-trained
- he's quiet and shut down
- he doesn't want to interact with 'his' new people at all.

From the dog's point of view any or all of these behaviours are completely understandable. And most professionals will tell their potential clients about the rule of threes (see page 41). Any adult dog has a set of often-unknown experiences behind him – he comes with baggage and it's bound to take some time to unpack.

▶ **Into the unknown**
A new dog is unlikely to behave characteristically in his first few days in a new home. He needs time to balance up his previous experience of life and find how it fits in with his new surroundings.

THE RULE OF THREES

The rule of threes says that it will take three days for a dog to take in new surroundings and to begin to relax, three weeks to realize that this is where he seems to be going to stay, and three months to settle in and to accept that he's home. The first two stages may trigger uncharacteristic behaviour, and it's often only in the third stage, at the three-month point, that things will settle down enough for you to understand who your new dog really is. Of course, these aren't hard and fast timings – a new dog may remain quiet for a week, may play up after two, and may only really settle down for life after six months or even more. But the rule of threes can help you keep things in perspective with a new dog.

▲ Arriving

It's a good idea to keep things as calm and consistent as possible with a new dog, and to settle him into a regular routine of meals, exercise and rest. Over his first few days with you, your new dog may behave in ways that don't turn out to be characteristic in the long term. Quite often new dogs are very 'good' and subdued over their first days in a new home because they're unsure of themselves and of what's expected of them.

▲ Habituation

At some point, usually two or three weeks after his initial 'good' – or even 'too good to be true' – behaviour on arrival, a new dog may start to feel safer and to 'let down his hair'. This may mean anything from stealing socks, being more demanding about what he is or isn't allowed to do, or indulging in 'riskier' play. Sometimes it seems to new owners that the dog that initially settled in so well has taken a step back, but the truth is that he is probably beginning to relax.

▲ Settling in

After three months, you'll be starting to get an idea of who your dog really is as he starts to relax into his surroundings. Some experts believe that it may take anything up to a year for a dog to fully unpack his concerns and settle into a new home, owner and life, but by the three-month point you will certainly be getting used to one another's likes, dislikes and personalities.

HOW TO HELP YOUR DOG
TO SETTLE

Of course, some adult dogs bounce into their new homes without a backward glance, enthusiastically greet everyone they meet and settle down into their fresh routine without problems. But if yours isn't finding it quite so easy, don't worry there are ways you can help.

PREPARE IN ADVANCE, THEN LET HIM INVESTIGATE
Set up your dog's sleeping arrangements, whether a dog bed or a crate, where he can see what's going on, but away from any activity. A corner of the sitting room or kitchen will usually work. Make it comfortable, and if possible add a blanket or other bedding that he's already used to, so that he has a familiar smell as a comfort.

ALLOW HIM TO EXPLORE
It's usual for a new dog to explore every inch of his surroundings. He uses his nose as you do your eyes to tell him where he is and to acclimatize himself to his new space. Don't try to distract him with attention or toys while he's doing the vital work of smelling out his boundaries, and be prepared for this to take quite a long time.

MARKING HIS SURROUNDINGS
He may 'mark' (pee a small quantity) as he explores. If you catch him in the act, say 'uh-uh' and take him outside. If you don't, just clean it up. It's a behaviour that's likely to stop after a few days – it's not necessarily an indication that he isn't house-trained. Whether he marks or not, you should take him outside every hour or so – in addition to his walks – for the first few days and praise him warmly if he performs while he's out there.

▼ **Let him eat and sleep**
Feed your dog in a corner of the kitchen, and once you've put the bowl down, leave him to eat in peace, without an audience. The same goes for sleeping: when he settles down, leave him alone. Don't surprise him in his basket when he's dozing, and don't loom over him or crowd him when he's resting.

KEEP THINGS CALM

Even if a new dog isn't calm, stay calm yourself. If he barks, don't respond by shouting. Talk to him in a cheerful, even voice. Let him initiate contact and come to you for any fuss – don't force it on him and don't allow anyone else to bother him. When he does come to you, fuss him calmly and keep your hands where he can see them: try a gentle scratch under the chin, for example. If there are places he's sensitive about being touched, this approach will let you know where. You'll know you're winning when he rolls over for his first belly rub.

▲ Taking his time

The best thing you can do for an unsettled dog is to let him take his time, and choose his own safe space and (within reason) activities. Engage with him when he comes to you, but don't hassle him for affection he may not yet be ready to give.

BE CONSISTENT

Make sure everyone in the house takes the same tack. If there are house rules, everyone must follow them. Consistency is key in helping him to feel secure.

If this sounds like a long list of 'don'ts', there's a reason for it. The easiest way to help a dog to feel safe and to begin to settle in new surroundings is to allow him to take them at his own pace. And the most common mistake new owners make is to extend a very effusive welcome that has the opposite effect to what was intended by making the new arrival feel crowded and nervous.

DOG'S-EYE VIEW

TIME TO SETTLE

It was hard to arrive somewhere where I didn't know anyone, and at first new people kept arriving to meet me and I felt shy and uncertain. Gradually the main people in the place seem to have understood that I need space and time to get used to everything. They set me up a decent den from the beginning, with lots of blankets to hide away in, and they let me spend time there without bothering me, which made it easier for me to relax. Two weeks in I've started to enjoy my walks and the fact that we always come back to the same place. I've spent some time on the sofa without anyone shooing me, and I've had a few games with the people here. I'm starting to feel safe.

43

MY DOG IS DIFFICULT TO
HOUSE-TRAIN

Many dogs are house-trained as puppies, and never have another accident in the house. But what if you have a new dog who has never been effectively house-trained? Or a puppy who doesn't seem to be getting the idea? Or a rescue dog, and you just don't know whether he's house-trained or not? Whichever dog you have, assume you should start from scratch. It will soon become obvious how far along the house-training road the new arrival is, and you can adjust the schedule accordingly.

THE HOME IS HIS DEN

Dogs originally lived in dens, not houses. They didn't toilet where they slept, in the den. So a dog needs to understand that, for a human, the whole of 'inside', whether it's a large house or a small flat, counts as the den, and he needs to go outside. House-training is the process of teaching him this, whether he's a puppy, an adolescent or an adult. It's straightforward; how long it takes usually depends on how meticulously you follow the steps with your dog (and, to some extent, how old the dog is). To house-train effectively you need to be in the immediate vicinity of your dog most of the time.

▶ **Spot the signs**
Even puppies show some signs that they're ready to go. And adult dogs tend to pace and circle – they don't just pee with no warning. Ideally your dog should be going outside so frequently that he doesn't get the chance to pee indoors, but it helps if you're savvy enough to spot when an accident might be imminent.

▲ Deal with setbacks

Almost every dog can be house-trained with patience and persistence, but initial constant accidents can be discouraging, particularly with a grown dog. Clear up calmly and completely ignore accidents unless you catch him in the act – in which case a quick 'hey!' or 'uh-uh!' and a speedy ushering outside will help to get back on track.

DOG'S-EYE VIEW

A PLACE TO TOILET

I prefer to pee and poo in the same place, just like people do – but unlike you, given the proper signs and opportunities, I'd prefer to go outside, well away from where I eat and sleep. And, unsurprisingly, I like to be sure I won't be interrupted or disturbed. A quiet corner, preferably with some undergrowth cover works best – and once I've fixed on it, I like to go back to the same spot most times because it smells right. When I was learning, my human used to lead me there; now I've got into the pattern, I'm perfectly able to find my chosen place for myself.

MY DOG IS DIFFICULT TO HOUSE-TRAIN

HOW TO START A HOUSE-TRAINING
PROGRAMME

You need to take your dog outside frequently. Small puppies will need to go at least once an hour during the day if you're to avoid too many accidents (they don't have the bowel and bladder control to wait very long until they're older). Adult dogs can wait longer in theory. But if they don't really understand house-training, or no-one has ever trained them, the fewer accidents they have indoors, the quicker they will get the idea.

OUTSIDE

When you go out with your dog, be out for a while, so that he has the chance to sniff the ground and wander about a little. Stay with him (don't stand by the back door), and walk around yourself, so he's not just waiting for you to go back in so that he can, too. If he performs, praise him warmly, give him a treat and take him back inside. If he hasn't done anything after five minutes, despite sniffing and wandering, take him back inside, but bear in mind he may need to go back out quite soon.

▶ **More than one dog**
Dogs learn from each other, so if you have a reliably house-trained dog already, a second dog will pick up the rules extra quickly, provided that both are encouraged outside often enough. But, bear in mind that a non-house-trained dog may not initially be able, or willing, to 'hold' it for as long as a house-trained one.

INSIDE

If your dog pees or messes indoors and you don't see him do it, clean it up without saying anything or tutting (if he senses disapproval, next time he may still go in the house, but hide). Smell plays a big part in where dogs choose to toilet, so use a specialist pet-shop product, rather than standard cleaning materials; these mostly contain ammonia, which may encourage a dog to pee in the same spot again.

LOOK FOR THE SIGNS

If you see your dog begin to turn in circles and to sniff the ground, both signs that he needs to go, take him straight out before he has an accident. If he begins to squat in front of you, say a short, sharp 'Hey', and run with him to the back door. If he manages to land even a drop outside, praise and treat as usual. Run out with him and encourage him along, but don't carry him – when he needs to pee, it's even more important that he learns to get there for himself.

OVERNIGHT

Although dogs don't need to go out as frequently in the night as during the day, it's likely that a puppy may need to go out once or twice and an as-yet unhouse-trained adult may need to go at least once, too. Your dog will wake up and may cry or whine, so he needs to be sleeping near enough to you for you to hear him. The most sensible solution for a dog-in-training is to have him sleep in a crate in or near to your bedroom, then you won't sleep through a need-to-go-out wake-up call. Get up and go out and wait with him, and praise and treat when he goes, just as you would in the daytime.

TRAINING OLDER DOGS

Begin by taking an older dog out as frequently as you would a puppy, and leave longer gaps if it becomes clear he doesn't need to go quite so often. Bear in mind that your dog is more likely to need to go straight after he wakes up, after he eats and after activity – for example, if he's been playing an energetic game.

▲ Watch the signs

As a dog starts to get the idea, he may move from sniffing the ground or circling to actively trying to attract your attention or going to the door when he needs to go out. Watch out for the signs, praise him warmly and get him outside fast.

47

HOW LONG WILL HOUSE-TRAINING TAKE?

This is a real 'that depends' question – and one of the things it depends on is following the process to the letter. An adult dog will usually have house-training in place, allowing for some accidents, after two months. A puppy may not be reliably trained before he is between eight and ten months old – some breeds seem to be slower to train than others, but most don't have complete bladder and bowel control much under ten months.

The best-case scenario is that there be someone at home with your dog all through the house-training process. If this isn't possible, try not to leave your dog alone for more than two hours, in a crate if he's crate trained or in a confined part of the house behind a baby gate if not. If he's left so long that he has an accident, it will set back house-training.

24-HOUR CYCLE

If you're uncertain about how often a dog might need to go out, consult the 'wheel of house-training' below. This isn't prescriptive (you'll have your own jobs for the day), but it does give you an idea of what might be typical while he's still learning to be clean in the house. Much like people, dogs don't usually need to go as frequently during the sleeping hours, although if at first you have frequent accidents, you may need to add in one middle-of-the-night break. Otherwise, allow for every hour or two at first (not as frequent as it sounds, given that he'll be having walks and play breaks in any case) and bear in mind if he's been outside without peeing, you may want to make the next break sooner rather than later.

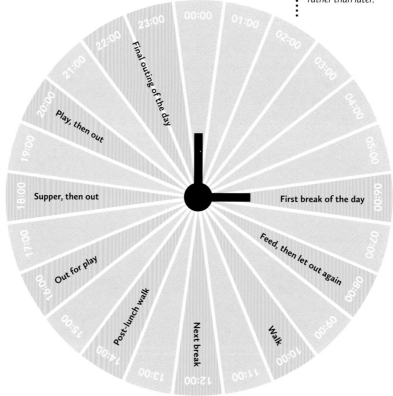

WHEN HOUSE-TRAINING BREAKS DOWN

If your dog was house-trained but he keeps having accidents, a vet check should come first to make sure that there isn't a physical problem. Older dogs can become incontinent, in which case there are various drugs that the vet may prescribe, or some natural herbal alternatives, including agrimony and raspberry leaf, that may be effective.

There's also the possibility that some peeing 'accidents' aren't really accidents – for example, a dog who is house-trained but in new surroundings may pee small quantities to 'mark' (see page 42), a behaviour that's likely to disappear when he is settled. Equally, a dog that is especially submissive may pee a little when greeting you – again, this isn't related to house-training, but is a completely different behaviour that's most likely to stop if you build his confidence up.

▶ **Peeing problems**
If house-training continues to be a problem long after you've followed all the rules, and even when your dog has plenty of opportunities to go outside, it's worth checking that there's no other problem, such as a bladder infection. Elderly dogs, too, may sometimes become incontinent when they've always had solid house-training. If either of these is a possibility, seek advice from your vet.

MY DOG CHARGES
AT THE DOOR

This is probably the most common problem of all: your dog barges and barks when someone comes to the front door, and either rushes out when it's opened or mugs visitors as they arrive. What you want is a dog who stands back as the door is opened and comes forward to greet people politely when they're in.

LEARNING THE CUES

There are several steps to the process, but you can teach your dog good door manners with two cues:

- 'Sit'
- 'Stay'

When someone comes to the door, instead of telling him not to do things, you give him something else to do – stay back and sit down.

Your dog is going to sit some distance from the front door and stay there through a series of increasingly exciting developments – from a ring on the doorbell, to the door opening, then people coming through it. Only when they're in the room is he going to be 'released' to come forwards and greet them. To teach him all this, you'll need a partner to ring the doorbell on cue, probably many times, then greet your dog calmly when they get through the door.

This is one of the most challenging exercises you can ask of an excited dog, so practise his stay before you start, and go on practising, gradually moving a little further away from him and asking him to hold it for a little longer each time, until he can reliably do it. When you're confident that he can hold a stay without distractions, you can start the full exercise. There are a number of stages and each one may take a few sessions for him to master, so reckon on the full sequence taking a while to teach.

▲ Dog dashing

The front door is a flashpoint for most dogs – and plenty of research has been done into why. It's been found that feral dogs aren't territorial in the same way about their 'found' areas, so some experts have speculated that it's actually our human interest in the entry/exit points of our houses that make them so fascinating for dogs.

DOG'S-EYE VIEW

DOOR APPEAL

The front door's almost the best part of the house: it's where everyone arrives, and I can sniff and greet them, plus it's where the post gets delivered (and I can make the postal worker go away just by barking, I've found). It's also one of the smelliest spots in the house – all the people who've come in and gone out leave their scent molecules on the threshold, and even when I've been out myself, I can smell they've been there. It's almost (though not quite) as good as the kitchen. And humans seem to be just as interested in it as I am.

MY DOG CHARGES AT THE DOOR

HOW TO TEACH THE
DOOR SEQUENCE

Work through the stages quite slowly and make sure your dog can hold his stay through each one before you move on to the next. It may take several sessions to teach this successfully.

Stand facing your dog in his position across the room from the door. Ask him to sit, and then to stay. Have him sit on a dog bed or a cushion and leave it in position during every session – it gives him something concrete to go back to. While he holds his stay, walk across to the front door, then back to him, and give him a treat. (If he follows, say 'uh-uh' and begin again.) Repeat until he knows that when you walk back to him from the front door, he'll get a treat if still in a stay.

Now, ask a partner to ring the doorbell gently (not too loud or long; it will be exciting enough for your dog as it is). Ask your dog to staaay, using a long, low tone (the calmer it is, the less likely he is to leap up). He probably won't manage it the first time, and it may take several tries, but keep going (across several training sessions if necessary), until he is staying in place when the doorbell rings. When he does it, walk back and give him a treat (don't open the door yet).

SEQUENCE LEARNED

Ask your dog to stay until the visitor is fully and safely in and you have shut the door. After that, it's a question of practice. Go through it every day, with staged visitors, and at times when you're not near the door yourself. If your dog starts to break his stay stage, take the sequence back to an earlier step and start again. Be patient. Eventually, rather than rushing to the door when he hears the bell, your dog will go to his stay spot instead.

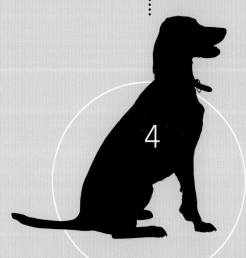

The next stage is to open the door after the bell rings. Open it just a crack, so that your dog can't yet see the caller. The moment the door opens is often the trigger for a dog to leap forwards to see who's there, so go through another stage – opening the door just a bit and then closing it again – before the final stage: the door opening and the visitor stepping into the house.

MY DOG'S UNSURE
OF STRANGERS

Why are so many dogs wary of strangers? Does it go all the way back to when they were puppies? If they'd been socialized a little more widely, would they be equally relaxed around all humans? So often, it's fear that takes us into unknown territory with our pets, and it's frustrating to realize that we can only speculate as to what causes the fear.

A lot of research has been done into the canine fear of strangers, and there are specific aspects of strangers that we now know dogs don't like. Dogs don't understand removable parts: a familiar person in a hooded parka may be treated exactly like an unfamiliar person until they take it off (even when a dog sniffs them, he still apparently can't reconcile the familiar scent with the unfamiliar appearance). The same goes for sunglasses – even on a familiar face. Dogs are also more worried by unknown men than unknown women – and again, this has been tracked back to the way they move rather than something more 'male' about the way they smell.

Can you turn the wariness around by tackling individual triggers that seem to signal 'stranger danger' and conditioning a dog against them? It seems that in some cases you can, and in others, the fear, or perhaps sensible caution, outweighs any positive spin you can set against it.

▶ **Stranger danger**

It's not really useful to go endlessly into how a dog became wary of strangers in the first place, but it is worth trying to identify the specifics of his fear. The best way is to watch a situation closely where he becomes wary (without over-exposing him to what makes him fearful). Is it every stranger in most situations, for example, or only men, or only men in hats? When you know, it's easier to take action.

MY DOG'S UNSURE OF STRANGERS

HOW TO TACKLE YOUR
DOG'S FEARS

A timid dog may seem to be scared of all kinds of people, but it's worth trying to narrow down what it is that's frightening him. Noise? Unfamiliar outlines? Unwanted approaches? Then you can try to fix it. It's easy to keep people at a distance if you know that what's scaring him is someone looming over him at close quarters, and it's easy to have people throw treats without even making eye contact if you want to convey that strangers bring good things. If he's usually relaxed with people walking by, but suddenly started barking when the sun came out, is it sunglasses that he finds disconcerting?

▲ Someone standing
Body language can frighten a dog, as can unwanted attention from an unfamiliar source. Someone new should ignore a timid dog completely – no eye contact, no attempted petting – but throw a few treats in the dog's direction. And if they're indoors, it's better to sit down, at a distance from the dog, rather than to stay standing.

▲ Walking pair of people
If a dog seems fearful of people passing by, check out what they're wearing/carrying. Is it a hat? Sunglasses? A stick? Are they carrying something that's bulky, or an unfamiliar shape? One dog was fearful of workmen wearing knee protectors – at eye level they may have looked like enormous eyes. If a timid dog suddenly seems fearful of passers by, do all you can to increase the distance between them, then set up a few artificial 'passers by' situations where the dog is given treats at the moment he becomes aware of people (this means in the distance, rather than rapidly approaching).

▲ Crowd of people
Many dogs are intimidated by crowds, and it's unlikely that a fearful dog will change his mind on this one. If you want to familiarize him with larger groups of people, it's best to do so from a distance in big, open spaces such as parks. Don't put a fearful dog in a situation where he's crowded.

DOG'S-EYE VIEW

WHERE IT BEGAN

I don't like situations where new people come up to me and I feel I can't get away. It started when I was small and a big group of people came up and they were touching me on the top of the head where I couldn't see their hands. Then someone rolled me over and I felt really helpless, so I started to growl and they laughed at me, because I was only small. Ever since then, if someone I don't know well walks up to me, I growl. But people don't laugh any more; they don't seem to understand that I'm scared and I need them to back off.

▼ The lead

If you have a fearful dog on a lead, give him enough autonomy to back off. He needs to feel that he won't be dragged towards the object of fear, and even a tightened lead will send the wrong message. Keep it as loose and relaxed as possible.

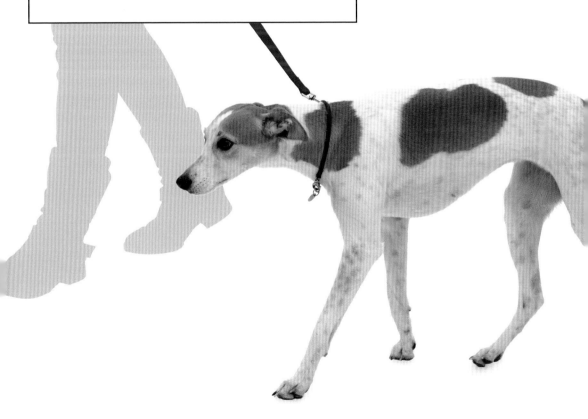

MY DOG IS
POSSESIVE

Most dogs at one time or another decide that they are reluctant to give up particularly valued items. If you train your dog to willingly give something up to you, knowing that he will always get something even better in return, you can often prevent him becoming too intense over what he feels is his.

Obviously this is useful if you ever need him to let go of something that isn't safe for him or that you really don't want him to have. Equally, it helps to keep him generally relaxed around the things he values: if he trusts you not to snatch things away from him, then he has less need to guard them. (*For concerns over more intense guarding and suggestions for ways to deal with it, see pages 100–101.*)

When you play 'fetch' with a dog who will bring the ball back but is reluctant to give it up for you to throw again, you take a second ball out with you, and throw that one instead. The dog will invariably drop the first ball and chase after the second one – which gained a whole new appeal as soon as it was thrown. Teaching him to play 'swap' works on the same principle: that the only reason he ever has to give anything up is to swap it for something better.

AROUND FOOD
Food is always a valued resource: one way to avoid your dog becoming defensive around his bowl is to put it down at dinnertime with only part of his meal in it. Wait until he's finished, and licked it out, then pick the bowl up again and put another small quantity in. If you do this, the lesson he takes away is that the only reason you ever pick up his bowl is to give him a second helping.

▶ Chase me

Don't make the mistake of getting into a chase game with a dog when you want him to give something up. It's better to turn your back and feign lack of interest than to turn it into a session of catch-me-if-you-can (you won't win).

DOG'S-EYE VIEW

MINE, MINE, MINE

You value your possessions, so it seems absolutely normal to me that I would value mine. And sometimes it's not clear to me why you would want me to give them up to you. Sometimes I steal socks because they smell good, but I get tired of them quite quickly. And even you would agree that most of the other things I lay claim to are mine. Sometimes you don't even seem to want them for yourself. However, if you offer me something just as good, I might be persuadable.

HOW TO LEARN
TO SWAP

You can set up a session of swap, or you can wait until the chance to play arises naturally. You'll need a good quantity of small but high-value treats and a toy your dog likes. The key is to turn it into a win/win situation for your dog, in which the end result of going along with your wishes is that he gets everything he thought he wanted and more.

1   To set up swap, choose a moment when your dog is relaxed and on downtime, and hand him his toy (if he doesn't always get interested on request, you can smear it with a little peanut butter, or intiate a game of tug with it, to make it more interesting). Give him a minute or two to engage with it.

2   Take several treats in your hand and hold it out to him, half closed, so that he can't grab them all in one go. He should turn from the toy to look at your more interesting option. If he doesn't drop the toy immediately, let one or two treats drop out of your hand, so that he can get to them easily, as an even greater inducement.

WHEN IT'S REALLY IMPORTANT

Nobody wants a possessive dog, but usually when he's guardy over a toy it's an irritation rather than an emergency. But what about when he's got hold of something that's really dangerous for him (picture your pet gnawing on the cap of a bottle of bleach, say). What's the right thing to do? Your best bet is to call his name (in an upbeat, super-bright voice) and run to the fridge. Grab something irresistible that he doesn't usually see much of – cheese, for example. And invite him to have some cheese, now, immediately. He's pretty likely to respond positively. Pick up the bleach bottle while his mouth is still full.

3 When he drops the toy and turns to the treats, let him take them out of your hand (keep it half-closed to slow him down). While he's eating, pick the toy up with your other hand. When he finishes the treats, hold the toy out to him so that he can take it back. Refill your hand with treats and play the game again.

4 If he's no longer interested in the toy, but only in the treats, give him a couple and end the game. After the first session, you can either set up further games of swap, or keep an eye out for opportunities to play at times when he's chewing on his toy anyway. And even if he loses interest in the original toy, always give it back to him as a last step in the game – the lesson he's learning is that he not only got something better than the toy he originally had, but that he got the toy back, too.

HOW TO LEARN TO SWAP

I CAN'T FIND A FOOD
TO SUIT MY DOG

We think of dogs as having cast-iron digestions, so it can come as a surprise if your dog is at the more sensitive end of the scale. The range of feeding possibilities is vast; although you should be able to sort out a regime for any dog, navigating your way around the choices can be confusing.

WHAT ARE YOUR OPTIONS?

There are three main options when it comes to choosing your dog's food:

- Commercially produced wet or dry food
- Home-cooked food
- Raw food

All have their pros and cons, and finding a diet to suit a sensitive dog can mean experimenting.

▼ Picky eater
Sometimes dogs are hungry but sensitive to specific ingredients. If he knows his food is going to give him stomach ache, he may be reluctant to eat. Always try a variety of foods with a fussy canine eater; don't keep pushing the same diet if he obviously isn't enjoying it.

COMMERCIALLY PRODUCED FOOD

Commercially produced food is the most widely used and exists in every imaginable combination, formula and price point. Owners who feed their dog on a commercial kibble or wet food or a mixture of both tend to find a brand that suits their dog and their budget and stick to it – which is perhaps duller than necessary for the dog.

HOME-COOKED FOOD

Home-cooked food needn't be more expensive, and is much easier to tailor around a dog's digestive sensibilities, but is obviously going to take more time to prepare. It needs to include protein (usually in the form of meat, fish and the occasional egg), fat, carbohydrate and vegetables. Owners are sometimes concerned that they won't get the balance right – and it's worth checking in with your vet about nutritional requirements (many will recommend an additional calcium supplement if you're going the home-cooked route) – but unless they cook the same ingredients every day, the natural variety of what they cook will ensure some balance in their dog's diet.

RAW FOOD

Finally, raw feeding does what it says: your dog is given raw food only, mainly meat with a fair mix of bones and organs. Some variations include additions of vegetables and sometimes grain, which will be cooked. There are commercial options, some organic, for raw-feeders too; you don't necessarily have to make up your own recipes or mixtures.

▶ Troughing in

The best result for an owner is seeing a bright-eyed, shiny-coated dog eagerly tucking in to a bowl of food that obviously suits him well. It's worth a bit of additional effort to get there.

DOG'S-EYE VIEW

HOW I EAT

The only way I can let you know whether or not I like my food is by eating it (or turning away). But don't expect me to take the same sort of time over my meals as you do. However much I'm enjoying the taste, I only do enough chewing to ensure that I can swallow it down. My digestion is significantly tougher than yours, so it will cope with what I give it, provided that my food isn't full of cereal filler, which isn't good for me and which gives me gas.

I CAN'T FIND A FOOD TO SUIT MY DOG

HOW TO FIND A DIET THAT
WILL WORK

Finding a diet to suit a sensitive dog can mean experimenting. As you'd expect, the cheapest food is rarely the best quality, so if you decide to feed a single complete product, whether kibble or wet food, buy the best you can afford and look for the simplest label: usually, the fewer the number of ingredients, the higher quality the food will be.

INGREDIENTS

In shop-bought food, specific ingredients ('chicken') are better than generic ones ('meat and animal derivatives'). However, even the better commercial food tends to contain additives, from preservatives to additional flavouring and colouring. If your dog has allergies (which may manifest themselves in skin problems) or if his behaviour is very hyper, blame for both conditions has often been laid at the door of highly processed food, so you may opt to go straight to the home-cooked or raw options.

If you cook for your dog yourself, you have complete control over the ingredients and can also feed a varied diet. Home-cooked food won't have the additives that act as triggers for some conditions, and it can be tailored to suit a dog with a sensitive stomach or allergies.

The raw-diet option has both fans and detractors. The fans prefer to feed their dog something closer to what they feel would be his 'natural' diet; those who don't like the idea worry about harmful bacteria being present in their dog's uncooked food. If you do decide on a raw diet, make sure that you buy meat from a reputable supplier.

WARNING

Never feed your dog any of the following; they're all toxic for dogs:

- Grapes or raisins
- Chocolate
- Macadamia nuts
- Onions or garlic
- Avocado
- Foods containing the sweetener xylitol.

◄ Chewing

Chewing for dogs is a valuable leisure activity: almost every dog enjoys it and it may be the closest that an active dog comes to a reflective hobby. Experiment with what your pet prefers to chew: many will enjoy a raw chicken wing, as well as the more commercial options like manufactured rawhide chews.

WHAT GOES IN...

'Digestibility' indicates the amount of the food a dog eats that passes into his system and that he uses – and the amount that passes straight through. Commercial food doesn't yet publish a digestibility percentage (more than 80 per cent would be considered a reasonable score), but the quantity of a dog's elimination gives you some idea: smaller and dryer stools generally indicate that he's getting the best out of his food; larger and softer ones aren't usually a good sign, suggesting that a relatively high percentage isn't giving him much nutritional benefit.

HOW DOGS EAT

A dog doesn't chew food as a human does; he gulps it, using his teeth only to rip it up and get it to a size at which it can be swallowed whole. Once down, his stomach does the digestive work. A dog's stomach is a very acid environment, killing off many of the bacteria that would make humans ill, which is why he can sometimes digest foods – such as near-rotten meat – that would make us sick.

THE BENEFIT OF BONES

Whatever they eat at meals, most dogs love raw bones – and bones are good for their all-round well-being, as well as their teeth and digestion. The bones must be raw, not cooked, and different sorts suit different dogs: if a hefty marrow bone doesn't seem to appeal, try him with smaller, easier-to-manage options, such as a raw chicken wing (also known as nature's toothbrush) or a rack of lamb ribs. Chewing is a major leisure activity that almost all dogs love and find therapeutic; it uses a complex network of muscles around the cheek and jaw, many of which never get a good workout otherwise.

MY DOG GOES FROM 0-60 IN
A NANOSECOND

He's lively and energetic and you love playing with him, but he gets overexcited very quickly and what was good fun for both of you is turning into jumping, catching clothing with his teeth, and even nipping on his part and increasing frustration on yours. How can you calm things down, and – in future – tone down his excitement so that it stops him from going over the top?

LEARNING HIS THRESHOLD

A trainer would say that a dog this excited is 'over threshold'. This means that he's so stimulated that he is shut down to anything other than the focus of his excitement. When you talk to him and he appears to ignore you, this isn't 'disobedience': he literally doesn't hear you because he can't take anything in.

At this level, he could be compared to a toddler who has tipped over from excitement and pleasure to hysterical-tantrum level. Don't feel that you're stopping his fun by teaching him to tone it down – actually you're calling a necessary break because he isn't having fun any longer: just like a toddler, he needs to learn to manage his excitement without tipping over.

Interacting with a dog when he's already over threshold isn't possible. You have to wait for things to calm down naturally (and if there's an obvious stimulus, like a toy, remove it altogether if you can), before you can begin to sort the problem. The aim is to keep his excitement levels under control by introducing some 'pause' signs as it rises. After a while, if you're consistent with him, a few seconds' time out and a change in focus every so often will keep things manageable and ensure that you can handle exciting situations between you.

▶ Tipping point

If your pet is naturally excitable, see if you can learn to judge the point at which he tips over – and call a halt to play well before the storm begins.

◀ Overexcited

When a dog is jumping and nipping, the best thing to do is to turn your whole body away from him. He's jumping to get nearer to your face, so make it unrewarding by presenting him with your back instead.

DOG'S-EYE VIEW

SAVING ME FROM MYSELF

When I get overexcited, all I can see is the toy or game I've been focusing on. The more I dash around, the more excited I get; and when I reach a certain point, I start to jump up and bark. Sometimes I might even nip, although I know you really dislike it. The odd thing is, that I'm not having much fun; it's as though the adrenaline has taken over and I just can't help myself.

When this happens, there's no point in getting angry with me. The most helpful thing to do is to ignore me. If we're outdoors, walk away from me and start to do something else; if we're in the garden, go indoors; if we're indoors, leave me and go into another room. Just leaving me will help, and you'll see that I can calm down, although it may take a minute or two. And whatever you do, don't shout at me: loud noises when I'm already feeling hyper will make me worse. And when we start to play again, a bit later, I'll be properly enjoying myself because you helped me take it down a notch or two.

HOW TO INTRODUCE
PAUSE TIME

Next time you play together, arm yourself with some treats as well as a toy and watch carefully as your dog begins to get excited. You're going to introduce some natural breaks into his play. Practise this regularly, and his self-control will begin to improve, so that he'll be better able to manage his own excitement levels, and won't tip into hyper behaviour so easily.

1   Well before he tips over, stop play suddenly and fast, put the toy behind your back and ask him to sit. Most dogs are so surprised at the sudden change in direction that they will react without thinking and sit.

2   The second his bottom hits the floor, give him a treat, then take the toy out again. Even the shortest pause will reduce his arousal level. Repeat through the play session, introducing pauses whenever you feel the excitement level is ramping up too high.

CALMING TREATMENTS

What if your dog generally has trouble calming down? If he gets plenty of exercise ('hyper' dogs are sometimes under-exercised dogs), but remains restless and seems to find it hard to settle, there are a couple of natural treatments that may be worth a try. DAP (short for Dog Appeasing Pheromone) was originally developed to mimic a natural pheromone that is released by a nursing bitch after she delivers her puppies. It makes the puppies feel secure; the theory was that DAP would have the same effect on an adult dog. It's available in the form of a plug-in room diffuser, as well as room spray and infused collars. Reports on its effectiveness vary: some users claim a strongly beneficial effect on their restless dogs, while others aren't convinced. Aromatherapy treatments for dogs are also becoming more generally available – practitioners offer a range of calming scents in concentrations pitched at a dog's very sensitive sense of smell. Again, reports on its effectiveness vary.

3 Eventually he'll start to pause, in expectation of the sit-and-treat, at the first sign you're moving the toy away and you'll have a way of lowering the excitement levels whenever you feel it's needed.

4 If at some point during the game he becomes excited and starts to jump up again and you haven't had the chance to prompt a pause and sit, turn your body away from him as he jumps up. This makes the jumping unrewarding and he will soon stop. As soon as his feet are on the floor, ask him to sit and treat him as soon as he does.

CHAPTER THREE

OUT AND
ABOUT

Being outdoors is exciting for a dog: more sounds, more smells, more to look at. And this can mean more headaches for owners – obviously everyone prefers their dog to behave politely at home, but when you're out and about, it's often actually necessary that he follows your lead. He needs to walk alongside you, he needs to come back when called, and he needs to be able to greet other people and dogs politely. So what do you do when your pet displays nil recall, or seems frightened of traffic noise, or behaves like a bully in the park? Here's how to work with him to fix it.

MY DOG PULLS AND WEAVES
ON THE LEAD

Surprising numbers of dogs never really learn to walk easily and happily on a lead. Some pull like trains, or constantly weave in front of you, or wander around in circles, tying their walkers in knots and appearing not to acknowledge that they're 'on the lead' at all.

RELEARNING LEAD WALKING

All dogs can learn to walk on a lead, and most have been taught at some point in their lives. But, lead walking is often something that needs to be taught again in adult doghood. This may be because lead walking never became an absolute habit, or maybe owners ignored it when their dog pulled or wove about, or maybe once taught it was never practised quite assiduously enough.

▼ Baffled and uneasy
Not all dogs pull on the lead; some have the reverse problem, just standing there, unwilling to go in any direction at all. If this describes your dog's approach, you will have to take some time convincing him that lead walking can be rewarding, with plenty of treats and interest along the way.

WHAT YOU NEED

Use a 2 metre (6 foot) lead to practise lead walking. Your dog should be wearing either a flat buckle or a fabric martingale collar or, for strong dogs that pull hard, a harness with a front loop to attach the lead (it will turn your dog slightly if he tries to pull). Don't use an extending lead – a dog that's enthusiastic about being out will always be at the far end of whatever limit you've set to the extender and you'll be sabotaging yourself before you start. At first, practise in your garden or somewhere else enclosed and safe, without distractions. Have an accessible pocket full of treats to hand, as you'll be using them a good deal at first. Fasten the lead to your dog's collar or harness, but don't take the other end – leave it trailing.

Look out for your own bad habits, too. You've been used to controlling your dog by pulling back at him, but now that you're aiming to have him walk willingly alongside you, you have to work at finding ways – other than brute force – of keeping him there.

▼ **Happy lead walking**
Ideally your dog should enjoy walking alongside you on the lead, without constantly veering off after new smells or other distractions. To achieve this, you've got to make lead walking fun. At the start, setting a brisk pace alongside your dog will help, too.

HOW TO MAKE YOUR DOG
LOVE THE LEAD

You may be surprised by how much concentration is needed on your part to teach (or re-teach) your dog to walk on the lead. Five or ten minutes will be long enough for your initial sessions (and at first, you'll simply be walking to and fro, or in circles). You'll need to keep an eagle eye on your timing, so you hand out treats at the exact moment – and sometimes it's only a moment – that your dog is doing just what you want, and not the one where he's beginning to do something else.

1 Most people like their dog to walk on their left side, with the lead held across their body in their right hand. So you need to attract your dog to your left side, and make it worth his while to walk next to you. Show him a treat in your left hand, patting your left leg. As he comes to you, give him the treat. While he's still looking up, on your left side, and paying attention, give him another one. Then walk a pace or two, taking out another treat. If he's still at your left side, give him the treat. If he isn't, pat your leg again – he doesn't get the treat until he's walking by your left side.

2 Next, make some turns, while still walking. Have a treat always ready, but make sure your dog only gets it when he's following on your left side, where you want him to walk. Turn around, double back, walk in a straight line, then turn and go in the other direction – but make sure that he only gets the treat when he's still close by on your left. Pat your leg if he starts to wander away from his position on your left, and treat him when he moves back there. On paper this sounds laborious, but you'll find you're kept quite busy, ensuring that he's in the right position, encouraging him back when he strays and dispensing treats with split-second timing.

3 Spend a few minutes once or twice a day practising this. When your dog is reliably at your left side and paying attention (for the next treat), pick up the loose end of the lead.

4 Carry on with the exercise, but holding the lead in your right hand. Try not to jerk or yank it – the principle should still be that your dog is sticking along by your left leg, at your walking pace (and following your changes in direction) while the lead remains loose.

Finally, add a verbal cue – most people use 'Heel' – as you treat. From this point, you don't do anything different, but you gradually phase out the treats (add plenty of praise instead), and practise in places where there are more distractions – quiet lanes or roads first, then busier ones.

DOG'S-EYE VIEW

SETTING THE PACE

We dogs don't tend to trot along side-by-side, especially not at the snail's pace you humans seem to prefer. When I'm out with my canine friends (off-lead, thank goodness), you'll notice that even when we're all headed in the same direction we circle and loop, joining up every so often to share appreciation of a particularly interesting smell. Not just that, but we go at a decent speed – I never thought that walking alongside you would call for so much patience on my part. What makes it worth it? Well, I have your undivided attention for our practice sessions, and there are plenty of high-quality treats on offer. You quite quickly realized that this wasn't going to be something I would do for a dry biscuit. And if I play it your way as we walk to the park, then the lead will come off and I can run around and sniff all I want to.

HOW TO MAKE YOUR DOG LOVE THE LEAD

MY DOG WON'T COME
WHEN I CALL

It's one of the commonest problems, and certainly one of the most complained-about among dog owners. You call your dog – the most typical situation is when you're in the park, he's mingling with a group of canine friends, and it's time to go home – and he won't come back. However often you call, he ignores you. He's gone selectively deaf. And when you finally go over to fetch him, thoroughly exasperated, he doesn't really get it – he comes away from his friends reluctantly. You're cross. You know you shouldn't, but you end up shouting at him. And, of course, that isn't going to encourage him to come back to you next time, so it turns into a vicious cycle: you call, he doesn't come, you yell at him, even though you know it doesn't help... and so on.

How can you break the pattern and make yourself so attractive that he actually wants to come back to you, whatever other calls there are on his attention?

SHIFTING THE BALANCE

If you have an adult dog who has never had an effective recall, you need to be prepared to start again from the very beginning. This needn't be as daunting as it sounds. Set yourself up to win by practising somewhere where there isn't any competition at all for his attention. You know your own dog best, so set the bar as low as you feel is necessary for it to work, and choose a time of day when you think he'll be able to concentrate: maybe after he's already had a walk and burned off some energy, but not too late in the day, when he's tired or cranky. He's already learned that it doesn't pay off to come back to you, so the best way for him to unlearn this is to offer lavish rewards – treats, attention, fun – for, at first, very little effort on his part.

▼ **What you're aiming for**
Here's the attentive dog of your dreams – rushing towards you at the sound of his name, then waiting, eyes on yours, to see how he can help. For many owners, he's also the dog who's going to stay in your dreams unless you're prepared to spend quite a lot of time working on recall, step by step.

▶ Heedless dog

… and here's where many people start: a dog who has somehow got used to doing what he likes, when he likes, as soon as the lead comes off. You're going to have to be very good fun indeed to make yourself more attractive than his other options.

DOG'S-EYE VIEW

WHY I IGNORE YOU

I was having a great time playing with friends (I'd done plenty of lead walking on the way to the park, so it was a relief when the lead came off). I tend to get absorbed in games of chase and wrestle, so I was surprised when my human came stamping over in a steaming temper: I'd simply never heard her call. And when she did arrive, she snapped on my lead and dragged me off. Bad mistake. Huge. Next time she turns up, I'll remember that's when the fun stops.

MY DOG WON'T COME WHEN I CALL

HOW TO GET MY DOG TO
COME BACK

A good recall needs to be practised until it's absolutely automatic on the dog's part, so set yourself up to succeed. This means making sure that in the early stages you're by far the most interesting thing on your dog's horizon. The good thing about the exercise is that it builds the closeness of your bond at the same time as teaching him to come back to you.

CHANGE THE LOCATION

If you have a garden large enough to run around in, start there. If you don't, choose a quiet corner somewhere your dog is already familiar with (park, recreation ground), at a time when no-one else – person or dog – is around, so that it doesn't offer any distractions. You need to be the most exciting thing there, so add to your appeal with favourite treats in hand, too – tiny cubes of cheese often work well. They should be so small that he doesn't have to pause to eat them; also, he's likely to be getting quite a few of them in the early stages.

HOW LONG WILL IT TAKE?

Aim to spend ten minutes per recall session, but make time for one every day. This may not sound like very long, but it's more important to keep them frequent and regular. That way, neither of you will get bored, and the sessions themselves – with attention, games and treats – will quickly become something your dog looks forward to. The only reason ever to skip a session is if there is a day when, for whatever reason, you're in a bad mood yourself. Your attitude will communicate itself to your pet, so you need to be relaxed and upbeat; if you're enjoying yourself, the chances are that he will, too.

▲ **Following a scent**
Remember just how much stronger your dog's scenting sense is than yours. Studies have shown that a keenly scenting dog may be literally deaf to anything else. He may not even have heard you call.

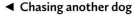

◀ **Chasing another dog**
Or, even worse, a squirrel. Whether he's in the middle of a chasing game or in pursuit of a small furry animal, he's highly unlikely to stop dead in his tracks. You'll have to wait for a natural pause to get his attention.

The most common mistake in training is stopping before the behaviour you want has become absolutely habitual to the dog. Expect this to take weeks, or even months, not days, and make sure you practise recall every single day, even if it's sometimes only for a few minutes a day. You're aiming to form a habit that is going to seem completely natural to him, and this will take time: after all, if you're teaching an adult dog, the bad habits took a while to learn, so the good ones will, too. Even when he's reliable about coming back, practise at times when your dog is not distracted and you don't actually need him to come to you. Recall is a lifelong skill: make sure he keeps it well honed.

OVERCOMING DISTRACTIONS

Set yourself up for success by only calling your dog when you are certain there's at least an 80 per cent plus chance that he'll return to you. Not many dogs have absolutely 100 per cent reliable recall, but you can work on getting it as close as possible by calling him only when you and your excellent treats are the best thing within range. Over time, recall may be strengthened as it becomes habitual – the more he does it, the more he's likely to do it – but getting the 'habit' started is down to you. Think carefully about calling him – are you going to be more interesting than what he's doing? If you've practised the exercise on the following pages plenty of times but the honest answer is 'no', wait until he comes out of his absolute concentration on something else before calling him.

▲ Absorbed with a toy
Unless you have a toy he values even more highly about your person, he may be concentrating too hard to rush back to you. Sometimes an offer to join in the play may work in this situation.

◄ Playing
If he's mid-game, your chances aren't good. You could wait for a natural pause, or enlist another owner or two to call your dogs to you together: if you can catch the dogs' attention as a group, the chances of them coming over together for a treat are better than those of getting a single dog to come back.

1 It's a terrible idea to turn chasing your dog into a game; getting him to chase you, on the other hand, is an excellent foundation for good recall. Almost all dogs love a game of chase, and most will be as happy to chase as to be chased.

Start by calling his name. As soon as he looks at you, hold up a treat. He'll move towards you and, when he reaches you, give him the treat, take out another, and turn and run away from him. He'll chase after you – and the treat. Repeat, treating him whenever he catches up with you, and constantly changing direction, doubling back, then setting off again.

(The changing direction and doubling back will be important to keep you ahead of him, as few people can run as fast as a determined dog!) That's all there is to it, but make sure you keep it fun and light-hearted.

2 Very gradually change the pattern so that you're giving out fewer treats, but replacing them with plenty of praise and fuss. Introduce other elements into the routine – if he loves playing ball, for example, bring a tennis ball and bounce it in front of him, then run away again, throwing it for him when he catches up with you. Every so often, stand still rather than running away, and, when he reaches you, make a huge fuss of him. Gradually reduce the chase element and increase the fuss element – the end result you want is for your dog to come back to you while you're standing in one place.

3 Some dogs will extend the fun by running around you when they come back. While this may be fine within a game, when you call a dog it's often because you want to put him back on his lead, so introduce an extra step: as he arrives back with you, say 'Sit!' in an upbeat voice (time it so the instruction comes exactly as he arrives back with you, and is focusing on you) and, as he sits, gently reach for his collar and give him a treat at the same time. Go gently (no dog likes being grabbed by the neck) and at first hold the collar for just a second and then let go. Over many repeats, build up first to clipping the lead on (leaving the other end loose), and eventually to clipping it on and picking up the other end. Even if you're in your own garden, say 'Let's go!' when you reach this stage, and walk up and down with him on the lead for a minute. You're keeping it fun for your dog but as you do, the sequence will be becoming more and more familiar and habitual.

4 After a while – and remember, it's more likely to take weeks than days for him to come back every single time – change the location to somewhere slightly more stimulating or unfamiliar. Set him up to succeed: don't skip stages and go straight to the park where all his friends hang out – instead, try a friend's garden or practise in the course of a walk. Step by small step, you will have brought him around to the idea that when you call his name, it's the start of something interesting, and that it will always be worth coming back to you.

MY DOG'S SCARED
OF ROAD NOISE

To noise-sensitive dogs, loud traffic or some of the individual noises within it – air brakes, motorbikes revving or cars backfiring – can act as a powerful stimulus to various kinds of fear-based reaction. Your dog may lunge and bark, shrink back, freeze very still or try to escape. The fear makes both you and him miserable and also means that walking alongside a busy road is nearly impossible. How can you help him to deal with his concern, and teach him that there really isn't anything to be afraid of?

HEADING OUT OF TROUBLE

Before you can start to help him, you need to establish the threshold at which the reaction starts. As with overexcitement (see pages 66–69), he'll only be able to respond to something positive when he's not reacting to something negative. If this sounds a bit convoluted, just think of how difficult it is for you to take something in when you're feeling apprehensive or fearful. Only when he is below the threshold at which he starts to feel fear can you begin to desensitize him to the noise, and this means starting when he's altogether out of earshot of anything that will worry him.

▼ Reactions to fear
Learn to recognize signs that your dog is afraid. Ears back and down is usually a sign of apprehension; a tail tuck, under the body, moves the body language into fear territory. A closed mouth with tight corners can mean your dog is feeling fearful, too.

FIRST CHOOSE YOUR ROUTE

This calls for good observation on your part. Choose a walking route that starts in a quiet place and gradually takes you closer to a busy road: the situation in which your dog is frightened. Then watch him closely to pinpoint the moment in the walk at which he starts to register concern. The signs may be tiny – he might prick his ears very slightly as he begins to hear distant traffic, or his tail may change from a relaxed swing to something a little tenser. As soon as you notice the smallest sign of stress, well before he's showing fear, note where on the road you are, then walk him back the way you came.

TURNING THINGS POSITIVE

As usual when you want to reinforce one thing and play down another, have a pocketful of small but high-value treats. Walk the route you picked that takes you towards traffic, remembering where he began to show concern before, and keeping a close watch on his body language. Slightly before you reach the spot, or sooner if you spot any tension at all on his part, give him a treat. Just treat him and keep walking, don't ask for any specific behaviour. As before, as soon as he shows even the smallest awareness that you're getting closer to the road, treat him. After the treat, turn around and retrace your route.

BABY STEPS

Desensitizing and counter-conditioning may take some time to work, but combining an extremely limited exposure to whatever your dog is afraid of (in this case, heavy traffic) with something he enjoys (treats) should gradually transform his fear to an anticipation of something good happening. Once he is looking to you for the treat at the point on a route when he was previously beginning to show apprehension, you're winning. Aim to go a little further along the route each day, even if it's only a few metres, treating your dog as soon as he looks to you, and turning long before he's showing anything other than anticipation of a treat. Very gradually, anticipation will win out over apprehension and he'll be able to hear traffic noise without fear.

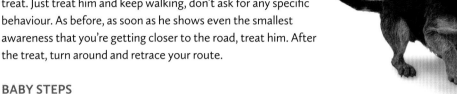

▲ Taking the initiative
Some dogs show fear by backing off and using their body language to make them 'small'; others, though, react to things they're frightened of by lunging and barking – a kind of 'I'll get it before it gets me' approach. Your job is to prove that you're his protector, and that you won't lead him into situations that are difficult for him.

THE FEAR FACTOR

Fear triggers in dogs aren't fully understood, and there's no definitive answer yet as to why one dog can trot happily alongside even the noisiest traffic, while another may be scared silly. There's a theory, though, which says that it depends on factors when puppies are in the womb. If a pregnant dog is in a state of regular stress and is producing consistently high levels of cortisol (the hormone associated with anxiety), her puppies seem to develop fewer cortisol receptor cells. While this may be helpful before birth, afterwards the low number of receptors can mean that a puppy's system has to be overloaded before the cortisol is registered at all. The result will be that the puppy, and later the adult dog, may go straight from a calm state of mind into something approaching pure panic, even in a situation where mild anxiety might seem more appropriate.

HOW TO HEAR NOISE
WITHOUT FEAR

We've taken fear of heavy traffic as an example here, but the same approach can be used with most fears of something specific that you can approach or retreat from. The key is to give him something positive as soon as he becomes aware of the object of fear; as usual, timing is exceptionally important – even a fraction of a second too late and the fear will take over and he won't be able to concentrate. That's why it's especially important to choose the location where you're going to tackle his fear very carefully.

Your dog is aware of the object in the distance. Start the process by treating him as soon as you notice his awareness, then turning back.

C

D

This is the point at which the dog's awareness has increased, but fear isn't yet registering.

Work from D to C in very small increments. Just an additional step or two without a fearful reaction marks progress.

FROM FEAR TO GRADUAL ACCEPTANCE

If A is the object that your dog fears, at first you should advance towards it no further than point D (that is, you must stop at the point at which the dog first becomes aware of the object). Take your time working between D and C, as this may be the distance that takes the longest to overcome. Once the reinforcement penny has dropped, things often (though not invariably) move a bit quicker. Your dog's pace is the only pace here, though. It's impossible to give distances for these points, as they will vary from dog to dog – some dogs can get quite close the object of fear, but then react very suddenly and extremely, while others first become aware at some distance, then gradually grow more fearful. Observation is key, because this really does depend on the dog.

If this is the point at which, in the past, your dog has had a fearful reaction, your aim in the exercise is to gradually get him there, but without ever provoking that reaction again.

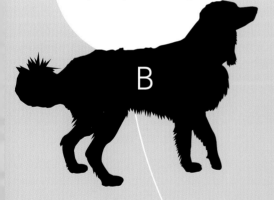

Eventually your dog may be able to pass directly by without a fearful reaction, but don't push it – it's better to have 30 visits with tiny advances but no reaction than it is to have 10 good visits and then to go too close and provoke a reaction on the 11th.

HOW TO HEAR NOISE WITHOUT FEAR

MY DOG DOESN'T PLAY WELL
WITH OTHERS

Maybe your dog tends to be pushy when playing with other dogs, and they try to avoid him? Or he acts as though he's frightened of dogs, hanging about on the edges of games as though he's scared to join in? Some dogs don't even seem to understand that they are dogs, rejecting play with other dogs altogether.

WORKING AT PLAY

Play for dogs is serious business. Many get most of their dog–dog social interaction through playing with dogs they meet outside their home, and it's a joy to see well-socialized dogs playing cheerfully together, chasing and wrestling and taking it in turns to 'win'.

▼ Taking turns

Most successful play for dogs depends on a turn-and-turn-about principle, with each dog taking different roles in sequence, just as it does with children. Within that basic rule, play styles vary a lot, but if you spend some time watching dogs play, you'll easily be able to spot the point at which the chasing dog becomes the one being chased, or the dog on top in a wrestling bout becomes the one underneath.

HOW I LIKE TO PLAY

Just like anybody else, I don't like to play with every single dog I meet. I've noticed that humans have their preferred people, too, so I doubt this is species-specific. I'm always a bit worried when another dog wants to spend a long time wrestling with me; I find the close contact makes me worried – I think they might forget they're playing, and I don't like being rolled around with the other dog on top. I think it's because I don't have a sense of control. Chasing, though, I can't get enough of; I don't really mind whether I'm chasing or being chased, but it wears me out (in a good way) and it's by far my favourite game. My two best friends like to play in exactly the same way: they chase me for a bit, then they'll pause and do a play bow, and the tables will turn and I'll chase them. My owner is good when I play; she doesn't interfere mostly, but if she doesn't know the dog I'm playing with, she'll keep an eye on me to see that I'm comfortable and that I'm having a good time, and if she spots I'm anxious, she'll call a halt (usually with a treat).

FEELING UNCOMFORTABLE

What about the dogs who aren't so comfortable with others, though? If there are signs that your dog isn't having such a great time, if he's looking stressed or overwhelmed, or, conversely, his body language is becoming highly aroused and his 'chase' with another dog is beginning to look more like stalking, what should you do? Is it safe to let them 'just work it out' between them, or should you play safe yourself and call your dog out the moment there's any feeling of tension in the game?

First, if you brought your dog to the park, you need to keep a close eye on him – especially if he's playing with a new dog. Should the game turn over-intense or if it's starting to look like a mugging, it's best that your eyes aren't on your phone. Trust your knowledge of your dog. If there are dogs he regularly plays with and they are already familiar with each other's play styles, chances are that this will be just another enjoyable play session. If your dog initiates play with a new dog, keep watching, but assume it will work unless you start to spot the signs of tension.

HOW TO SPOT AND STOP A
PUSHY PLAYER

Plenty of dogs don't need any help to play nicely – they just get on with it, enjoyably wearing themselves out with their friends. But just as in any playground with a range of personalities, some dogs get overbearing in play. If that's your pet, you need to learn, first to spot when it's happening, and, second, the right moment to call time out, so that things can calm down and stay good humoured.

DIFFERENT PLAY STYLES

Play styles in dogs can vary enormously, from evidently good-natured and straightforward-looking chasing to full-on roll-the-other-dog-over wrestling with accompanying growling and barking. If your dog isn't enjoying himself, or if he's beginning to act like the playground bully with another dog, he'll communicate it with his body language. Your knowledge of your own dog will tell you whether something playful is turning too intense, because you know his 'normal'; it's harder to tell with less familiar dogs, because signs such as hackles up, deeper growling or a slightly too-still body pose may still fall within their own play 'normal'. Rely on the signals your own dog's body language is sending, if you feel they look more intense than you're used to seeing, create a pause. From your dog's point of view, the worst you will be doing is stopping play for a moment or two. And if he was starting to feel either out of his depth or overexcited to the point of getting aggressive, you'll be doing both dogs a favour.

PUSHY DOG

Regular, good-tempered play between dogs is usually marked by frequent pauses – in a chasing game, for example, this will be when the chaser becomes the chased, or if dogs are wrestling, it may mark the point at which the dogs roll over and the one that was previously underneath gets his turn on top.

▼ Getting his attention
A short, sharp 'Hey!', and the offer of a treat, should be enough to distract your dog to get him to come to you. Just a momentary pause in play may calm him to continue play in a manner that's enjoyable for all.

A pushy dog may pause less often, seeming to make his own decision about when it's time for the game to change pace, without the body language 'consultation' that a pause, however momentary, can offer. In a chase game, he may begin to barge or body-block rather than chasing, or to nip at his playmate's neck or legs. In a wrestling game, you may spot that it always seems to be his turn on top. Just because he's a pushy player doesn't necessarily mean that the game is going to turn aggressive, but you may begin to see signs that the dog he's playing with isn't enjoying it as much as he is. These signs include:

- The head is turned away sideways
- The tail is level or tucked
- Your dog isn't letting the other one up straight after bowling him over.

If any of these are happening, it's definitely time for you to stage an intervention. If your dog has good recall, you will be able to call him over; if he's very excited or if he's distracted by the intensity of the game, you may need to give him a cue such as a sharp 'Hey!' to get his attention.

Often a momentary pause is enough to calm things down. If your dog comes over, praise him and give him a treat, then be quiet and see whether he goes straight back to playing – and if he's calmer when he does.

▼ Choosing time out
Dogs sometimes indicate a 'count-me-out' moment in play by turning away, sniffing the ground or otherwise absenting themselves from the action. Don't worry if he doesn't always want to join in; some dogs are happy spending more time doing their own thing, and prefer either one-on-one play with a close friend, or short periods of play with plenty of time out.

HOW TO LEARN TO RELAX AROUND
OTHER DOGS

What if, instead of being pushy, your dog is shy? Don't subject him to enforced socialization, especially not with a lot of new dogs at once: many dogs won't ever be truly comfortable at rush hour in the dog park. This doesn't mean that he won't play happily with friends, but introductions are best done calmly, one-to-one and somewhere there is plenty of space.

Play personalities sometimes need to be matched, too. A shy dog may play with a rambunctious one, but it should be his decision, and if you spot signs that he'd rather be elsewhere after a while (if, say, after a few minutes, he is still turning away, sniffing the ground and looking anywhere but at the other dog), he might prefer not to play today.

SOCIAL WALKS

An alternative way for dogs to get to know each other but with the pressure taken off is on a social walk. Keep the dogs on leads, and walk them parallel to one another but at a fair distance – around 5 metres (15 feet) apart. This gives a nervous dog the chance to settle down and be comfortable without any fear that the other dog will invade his space. As you walk, if they relax around one another, you can gradually allow the dogs to get closer and

▼ Staying close

Owners often feel they don't want to interfere in their dog's play. For a shy dog, though, it can be helpful to have breaks and short interactions with their owner. If you keep the tone casual and dole out treats freely, you can ensure you're a reassuring presence to build his confidence.

eventually to sniff in the same interesting spots, and, if there's no evident tension, to sniff one another and introduce themselves – but keep leads loose and keep moving. Trainers and behaviourists sometimes run social walks for groups of dogs, to offer the chance for nervous or under-socialized dogs to be in the company of other dogs without any risk of fear-created incidents.

USING A MUZZLE

Muzzles used to be seen as a last resort for an aggressive dog; recently, though, they've been much more widely accepted as a way to let nervous, sometimes snappy, dogs mix with others while preventing problems. Most dogs will learn to wear a basket muzzle (the open, cage type) quite happily if they're introduced to it carefully – owners often encourage their dog to eat treats from the muzzle, or smear it with a meat paste for him to lick off, to give it some positive associations. If you think you will have a more relaxed walk around other dogs if your dog wears a muzzle, try one out, and remember, it's not a badge of shame for your dog, it's the sign that you're a responsible owner. It's not an excuse for you to ignore your dog's discomfort, so continue to pay close attention to his body language and remove him from any situation that he's likely to find overwhelming.

▲ **Becoming independent**
Shy dogs may opt for low-key exploring sessions – sniffing in the undergrowth and sharing smells – with new acquaintances. This sort of casual interaction is great for a timid dog, as it reinforces social contact without being too full-on.

MY DOG DOESN'T WANT TO
GO FOR A WALK

When your dog has always been an enthusiastic walker, it can be a huge surprise when he suddenly prefers to stay at home. You wouldn't be surprised if he'd had a difficult encounter with another dog, or been frightened by fireworks, but as far as you know recent walks have been problem-free. What could be wrong, and how can you get him out walking again?

WHAT HAPPENED?

Dogs are rational and they have their own reasons, so he didn't 'just decide' that he didn't want to walk. If it came on suddenly – one day he was happy to walk and the next day he wasn't – rule out any possible health problems with a visit to the vet before you look for something more complicated. Dogs don't always display or complain about pain in the way people do, but it can be an underlying reason for odd changes in behaviour. If he gets a clean bill of health, though, you need to look for other potential causes. The most common one is that something happened that seemed insignificant to you but that spooked your dog. Sometimes if you think hard you'll find something that makes sense, but sometimes you'll never find the cause.

▼ Rule out illness
Do take an unwilling walker to be checked out by the vet to make sure that there isn't a physical problem. Dogs don't always make the sort of fuss you might expect when they're in pain.

WHY I DON'T WANT TO LEAVE THE HOUSE

I love walks, but a couple of weeks ago as we went out, a beam of light shone right in my eyes from the house opposite. I didn't know what it was doing there, and at first I ignored it, but it happened again the next time I went out and it made me feel really uneasy. Now I don't like going out of the front door. My owner doesn't know what's wrong; she's mentioned the ugly new security lights on the neighbours' house – they had them put in because they were burgled, apparently – but she doesn't seem to have connected them with me not wanting to go out of the front door. We reached a compromise; we go out of the back door, which bypasses that nasty beam.

▼ Think laterally
Sometimes a dog who won't walk from home will be happy to take a car ride to a walk. If he'll do this, try it for a few days to see if you can break the no-walk pattern.

HOW TO BREAK THE
NO-WALK HABIT

DOG DILEMMA
5
DOG DILEMMA

If you can't find a reason, try to find a way round the refusal. Don't ever force your dog to go out with the idea that he'll get over it once he's out of doors – it may simply add a fear of you and what you might do to his reluctance to walk.

FINDING A SOLUTION

Think of different ways of doing things. Take your dog out via a short car journey – even if you're going to the same park that you would normally walk to. Change your routine; try a walk at a different time, or use different preparations for a walk. Sometimes just altering cues and signals will be enough to 're-set' a dog's thinking. Make a game out of leaving the house – play all the way up to the front door and then out of it. Make the walk a positive-reinforcement exercise. Any or all of these may help to break the no-walk prejudice.

▼ **Try a toy**
If he's still enjoying playing out of doors, try starting a game in the garden, and then carrying it on to the start of a walk. Sometimes a favourite tug toy or ball may be enough of a distraction to get him over the first hurdle of going for a walk.

94

TAKING IT SLOWLY

If the friend/toy/enthusiasm tactics haven't worked, you can try the same technique as is sometimes used for separation anxiety – by taking the sensitivity out of the 'triggers' for a walk. This could mean taking tiny steps towards a walk but, for a while at least, stopping short before the walk itself.

For example, fetch his lead, put it on, then feed him a couple of treats and take the lead off again. Build up to the point at which you're putting his lead on and getting him to the front door, feeding treats, then taking his lead off again, then to the point of getting him through the front door, treating him and immediately going back in, and so on. Gradually you're building towards actually starting the walk, but in tiny increments. Leave it to him to set the pace, and never take him further than he's completely willing to go, or you'll reinforce his apprehension about walks rather than breaking it down. If treats aren't a major motivator for him, play with a toy can be an alternative. The key thing is that you're getting him, very gradually, to focus on what he likes and enjoys, and linking it to his walk.

▼ **Company may help**
If it's a confidence issue, he may feel happier walking with a friend. Arrange for one of his friends to come to the house, then leave for the walk together; having his mate step out fearlessly may help to break the pattern.

CHAPTER FOUR

WORKING
WITH WORRIES

If you've read through the first three chapters, you'll already have some ideas

of how to tackle various dilemmas and problems; here are a dozen more with

various techniques that may help to resolve them. Many of the solutions will

have more than one possible application – for example, you can use the steps for

reducing a toy obsession to work on other possessive problems, and the process

to stop your dog nipping will work if he insistently paws, too. The suggestions

should also encourage you to think laterally: is a problem always a problem if you

think about it in a broader context? What you'll find here should help you to build

your confidence working with your dog.

LEARNING BY PROBLEM
SOLVING

Dogs are fascinating subjects to work with, and this is as true if you're using your pet in your own problem-solving class of one as if you are studying behavioural characteristics in a public class with 20 other dogs and owners. Even those scientists who argue that a dog's 'personality' is simply a genetically generated list of traits that make up a working 'dog machine' still agree that one of the things that makes dogs so interesting is the fact that they are very different from one another.

EVERY PROBLEM IS AN OPPORTUNITY TO LEARN

The time spent working through problems with your dog can be used as an opportunity to learn more about him generally – that is, about his specific likes, dislikes, prejudices, enthusiasms and reactions to different things in different contexts. In this section, we focus on thinking around problems to find possible solutions, using each dilemma as a way to find out more about your dog and what works for him as an individual. For example, does a dog who hates his crate really need to use it? Can you persuade a sofa-hogging dog that it's his decision to get off the sofa? When you start thinking around problems, less-obvious solutions and possibilities may occur to you.

Neither owners nor dogs are machines – you may be good at teaching and your dog may be fast at learning, but there will be times when the dog just doesn't get it, and you can guarantee that it will be those times, as you try changes in direction and different ways to 'explain', that you'll learn the most about him. So use the suggestions as a template for problem solving, but be imaginative, too. And remember, you are the person who knows both your dog and your situation best, so you may also be the person to come up with the right strategy for your particular combination of circumstances.

STAY FLEXIBLE

The most important tool you can have in your training set is patience. If a dog isn't getting it, it may be that you're not explaining it properly to him. If that's the case, how might he understand? It's this attitude, rather than the inflexible application of a set of rules, that enables him to build his trust in you.

When you've successfully trained a dog away from an unwanted behaviour, don't abandon the exercise you used on the grounds that your dog is now 'cured' and the problem won't recur. Any professional will tell you that you should practise good habits, even if your dog shows no sign of regressing to, for example, being guardy around a toy. Treat practice as a small, enjoyable part of his daily routine.

▼ **Every one an individual**
The more all-around knowledge you acquire of dogs as a species, the more you'll understand and appreciate the degree to which your own dog is an individual within those species' limits.

HOW TO STOP
A TOY FIXATION

Your dog has been used to playing with a range of toys, but has become completely focused on one of them. Now he's almost given up playing with it in favour of guarding it. If there is anyone else in the room, he's constantly checking that no-one can take it. If someone approaches too close when he has it, he growls. It's called resource guarding, and there's a successful way to deal with it. Don't try to face down the growling and take the toy away, or tell him he's a bad dog – these won't work long-term: they'll result in him guarding even more fiercely. Instead, teach him that good things happen when someone approaches his treasure. You need treats (as usual, something he really loves, but in small pieces).

1

Stand at the door of the room where he's guarding his toy (if necessary, set the guarding situation up by giving him the toy in the room you're going to work in) and throw one or two pieces of the treats towards him.

DOG'S-EYE VIEW

LETTING GO

When I get hooked on guarding my toy, it feels a bit obsessive. Even though I don't like giving it up, in some ways it's a relief when my owner takes over the situation: it means that I can give up the responsibility of having to be in charge.

As your dog becomes familiar with the routine, he'll start anticipating your forward movement – he knows that as you come forwards, he'll get a treat. If at any point in the routine he takes up his guard, goes stiff or gives you a hard eye, start further away from him next time you practise: he will be setting the schedule here – all you have to do is follow it. When you're able to walk right up to him, practise reaching close to the toy (throw food), then touching the toy (throw food), then giving him back the toy. You only reach out and touch the toy when he's relaxed enough to let you do so, though, and how long this takes will depend on him. And when, eventually, you take the toy, you give it straight back to him to reinforce the fact that he gave it up – not only did he get something delicious, but he got his toy back, too.

Aim for them to land close enough so that he doesn't have to move to get them. Don't move towards him yourself, just throw the food. He'll snarf the treats up before settling back down to guard. Do this two or three times, then leave the room and put the food away. Repeat whenever you see him guarding. After a few sessions, take a step into the room before throwing the food. Wait till he eats it, step back to your previous position, then repeat – take a step forwards again and throw some more food. Every few times you practise, take a step further into the room before you throw the food. And always step back to your original position after you've thrown it.

HOW TO DEAL WITH
A BALL JUNKIE

You might wonder why this is a problem – he's outside, he's getting lots of exercise, and absolutely anyone can play fetch with him without having to do much running around themselves. But a complete obsession – to the point at which a dog can only focus on or think about this single activity – means that the dog can't concentrate on any of the other normal activities he would usually enjoy outside. And although it might appear he's 'playing' with the person who is throwing the ball, he's really on his own – so long as the ball gets thrown, it doesn't matter to him whether it's by a machine or a person; he barely notices which.

1 Dogs like this are nicknamed 'ball junkies'. Why? Because their behaviour in ball play has many of the qualities of an addiction – they think about it from the moment the ball comes out and they can't be distracted by any other activity, however appealing. The obsession gets even stronger when the dog is taken repeatedly to the same place, at the same time of day – it's a predictable ritual and in response, his anticipation rises higher and higher. Add the flat-out exercise he gets while retrieving – raising his adrenaline levels until he's even more excited and it's easy to see why his daily fix has become so important to him.

2   Change the pattern. Give him a session of ball-throwing every day, but change other things about it: play at a different time of day, use a variety of different balls and play in different locations. When you've played for 10 or 15 minutes, put the ball away and turn your attention firmly to something else. Bring other toys out with you, or have a quiet session of trick training with him, to help him calm down and use some mental energy.

3   If his ball obsession doesn't abate even though you're limiting him, he may have to go 'cold turkey' for a while. Sometimes the drive is just too great for him to be able to control himself. Hide the ball/s away completely and give him varied walks so that he can rediscover the joy of sniffing, exploring and just hanging out. Some owners find that introducing a session or two of raw-bone chewing into a dog's diet helps to limit other obsessions – no-one understands quite why, but it may be worth a try.

WHY DO SOME DOGS BECOME ADDICTED TO BALL PLAY?

The answer may be found in a dog's background – if he had an 'impoverished' puppyhood, lacking stimulation, one effect may have been that he developed fewer dopamine receptors in his brain. Fewer receptors mean an increased sensitivity to dopamine, one of the chemical 'messengers' in the brain. Dopamine levels are stimulated by reward-induced motivation (such as ball throwing) and seem to provoke very repetitive patterns of behaviour. So more play = more dopamine = more stimulation/obsession, and it quickly becomes a vicious circle.

LEARNING TO COPE WITH BEING
HOME ALONE

Dogs are social animals and very few like being left alone. Every owner has become used to the reproachful-eyes-at-the-door pattern when they leave their dogs. When a dog has separation anxiety, though, he becomes very stressed when left – and this can lead to a range of problem behaviours. Dogs may bark and howl for hours, pant and drool excessively (stressed dogs produce more saliva), damage things around the house or, in extreme cases, try to escape (gnawing at door and window frames, for example). In mild cases a dog may settle after a while; in more severe ones, he may be frantic the entire time he's left alone.

HOW TO HELP

If a dog suffers badly from separation anxiety, you may need professional help to overcome it. But in mild to moderate cases, there's a lot you can do to alleviate it.

1 Your dog knows a number of the signs that show you're going out, and they act as triggers for his anxiety. Think through everything you do before leaving (fetch your boots, take down your coat, pick up your keys and so on). Most people follow a particular order. If the first step in your process is to fetch your coat, for example, take your coat off its hook, give your dog a treat, then put the coat on its hook again. Repeat several times; your dog has watched you make the first step towards going out, he was treated and then you didn't go out after all. Do this several times a day. If your dog begins to anticipate a treat when you're taking the coat off the hook, you're starting to get results. Move on to the next stage (checking your keys, perhaps), and begin to treat that one.

2 Reduce his sensitivity to the signals that you are leaving by mixing them up and taking the predictability out of the sequence, so that he doesn't have the chance to work up to a high state of stress in advance. Leave your dog an activity toy, such as a food-stuffed Kong, but ensure that the actual moment of leaving is a non-event from your dog's point of view. Don't pet or console him, just calmly go. When you return, follow the same routine. Even if he's hysterical with excitement to see you, keep your greeting low-key and don't make a big fuss of him. The message you want to send is that your absence isn't a dramatic big deal.

DOG'S-EYE VIEW

A QUESTION OF RESPONSIBILITY

When you leave me, I don't know if you're aware of how I feel. There's no-one at home, and I feel responsible for the whole house – I can't relax until you come back. And I sometimes worry about what's happening to you, too: normally I'm in charge of looking after you, but when you're away, I can't even see you, much less be responsible for you. It's not surprising that I really don't like it.

HOW TO DEAL
WITH GRIEF

This is part of a much larger question: do dogs understand about death? And if a dog does grieve, is there any way of consoling him? For every owner who is convinced that their dog grieves in the same way that a person would, there's someone with a story about a dog who seemed indifferent to the death of another who had been his good friend. So it's safe to say that dogs don't all feel the same way about death.

1 Many people believe that a dog will only know that another dog is truly not coming back if he sees the body of the dead dog. It can sometimes avoid a dog undertaking a heartbreaking search for a friend who seemed simply to vanish – and it's not usually hard to arrange. Having some quiet time yourself with both dogs may help to deal with your own upset over the death.

DOG'S-EYE VIEW

GRIEF OR INSECURITY?

My owner believes that I'm mourning my friend, as I've been so much quieter since he died. Actually, it's the atmosphere in the house that I don't like; she's sad all the time, and now that he's not here to play with me, she doesn't play either, so I don't have any games or fun. I'm hoping she gets over it and becomes more upbeat soon, so that things can go back to normal and we can play again.

2 Afterwards, give it time. In this way at least, dogs are similar to people: they need some space to adapt to big changes in their lives. If your remaining dog seems sad and low, go along with it. Maintain his usual walks – exercise never hurts – and routine, and see if he perks up; get him checked over by the vet to rule out other problems if he's refusing to eat or is very lethargic. Try some additional one-to-one time with him, too, playing with toys or trick training.

3 If your dog usually likes canine society, offer him the chance to mix with other dogs by walking with friends or trips to the park. Don't immediately rush out and buy him a puppy 'for company': wait for at least a month before considering whether to add a new dog to the mix. If you ultimately decide it's a good idea, consider what age dog might work best and, crucially, what kind of personality/energy level would fit best into your existing situation. An elderly resident dog might love a puppy and find it gives him a new enthusiasm for life – but then again, he might prefer a quiet older rescue dog, or even no dog at all. It's a good idea to take him to some shelter meet-and-greets to gauge his reaction if you're thinking of going this route.

TAKING BACK CONTROL
OF THE FURNITURE

If a dog who has always been allowed on the furniture suddenly decides that the couch is for his exclusive use, and is demonstrating this by growling when you go to sit next to him, how can you take back control without confronting him? And why has he staged a takeover anyway?

What are your aims? You want the couch back, you don't want to be growled at and you don't want a face-off. The best approach is to manage a negotiated settlement in which your dog doesn't even realize he's being managed.

DOG'S-EYE VIEW

LOOKING TO THE LEADER

When I forget myself, my person is quite quick to remind me who's the leader. I don't really mind; he's my route to the good things in life, so when he makes me work for a treat, or dinner, or a walk, I'm happy to go along with it. A quick 'sit' or 'wait' are easy enough to do if it keeps him happy and gets me what I want.

Arm yourself with some high-quality treats that you know will have a strong appeal. Start when neither of you is in the room with the couch, call your dog and ask him for a simple sit. When he sits, give him a treat (so that he can see something exceptionally good is on offer).

1

YOU'RE IN CHARGE

As far as he's concerned, he's following a couple of simple instructions for high-value food. But you're actually reclaiming your couch. Keep practising daily, and close the door between times to ensure that he doesn't have the opportunity to climb up on the couch when you're not in the room. After a few sessions, you'll have established that he gets on the couch by invitation, and off it on request. Then all you need to do is to keep up the new habit with plenty of regular practice.

Stand up, walk a few steps away from the couch, and call him over. He'll get down and head towards you in anticipation of a treat. Treat him.

Repeat the on/off the couch routine several times, treating him each time he gets up and each time he gets off. If you've never used cues in connection with getting on or off the furniture before, now is the time to start. As you invite him onto the couch, say 'Up', as you ask him to get off the couch to collect a treat, say 'Off'.

Don't ever punish your dog for humping, or grab his collar to pull him away; instead, call or lure him away from the other dog, or ask the leg's owner to remove it from range as efficiently as possible while you try distraction tactics. A squeaky toy heard from another room, the fridge door opening or even the doorbell ringing are all possibilities for getting his attention without a huge amount of fuss.

2

3

109

HOW TO PREVENT
NIPPING

All puppies nip in play; their mother and siblings let them know when it's too hard, and they've usually stopped long before adulthood. But if a grown dog still nips, even when his intentions are definitely playful, his larger teeth and much stronger jaw can make a real impact on human skin if he uses any pressure at all biting down. You don't want to become an inadvertent chew-toy, but if he didn't learn to stop as a puppy, how can you stop him now?

1   First you need to make it unrewarding for him to carry on, then deflect him onto something else that will appeal to him and work better for you.

DOG'S-EYE VIEW

TEETH STOP PLAY

When I was a tiny puppy with my teeth through, and I used them inappropriately (or a bit too hard), the grown-up dogs around me ignored it at first. As I got older though, they warned me off quite scarily when I nipped, with lots of growling and tooth-baring, although they never bit me. It was noisy though, and it made me think twice. When I forget myself and nip now, the humans don't growl, shout or bite back: they turn their backs on me and won't play. And it works, because I absolutely hate being ignored.

2 Starting now, make sure that any kind of tooth contact with your skin stops play immediately – stand up, fold your arms, turn your back and walk away. Repeat as many times as it takes for the message to go in: if he's set in a pattern of nipping, you may find yourself stopping every play session at first, but he'll eventually get it.

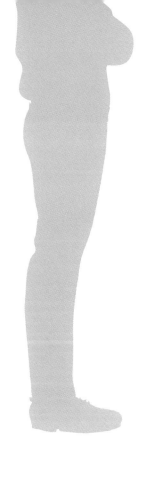

3 In the meantime, introduce a chew toy into play sessions – a rope tug toy or a stuffed toy, possibly one with a squeak to give it additional appeal, will usually work better than, say, a hard rubber toy, as he'll be able to sink his teeth in and shake it. When he grabs it, play with it alongside him, throwing it and playing tug with him, so that he gets the maximum play value out of it.

111

HOW TO HAVE A DOG-FREE
DINNER TIME

You weren't firm enough with your dog when he was younger; he was fed scraps from the table and now he's a confirmed presence at human mealtimes. Even if you ignore him, he stays close by with big, doleful eyes. And when you do get him to go away, he's there again the next time a meal's put on the table.

A few scraps of human food won't do your dog any harm, but as you've learned, it's fatal to feed him from the table. To unlearn the habit, you have to teach him that to get any of your food he has to do something that you want: lie down quietly at the other side of the room.

1 He'll learn this quickly provided you're firm and completely consistent (and everyone else at the table is, too). Sit out the begging first, until he gives up. This may take all of several mealtimes. If he's used to getting scraps from the table he may be quite persistent; don't scold him or ask him to go away – instead, ignore him completely. Ignore any attempts to get your attention, and don't speak to or even look at him.

2 Some dogs learn faster than others, but if it takes more than one mealtime, wait it out. Eventually he'll give up. At this point, most dogs will settle down in a corner of the room. As soon as he does, get up from the table with a scrap of food you've kept ready, and put it in his food bowl. It doesn't matter whether this is in the same room or a different room; the important thing is that it's the bowl he's normally fed from.

3 He'll follow you and eat it. If he starts mugging you when you return to the table, ignore him, just as you did earlier. When he lies down (he will eventually), take another scrap of food and put it in his bowl. Start by doing this every time he lies down, then gradually phase it back until his 'treat' goes in his bowl only when you've finished and are clearing the table.

HOW TO MAKE FRIENDS WITH THE
POSTAL WORKER

You've taught your dog to be polite at the door (see pages 50–53), but he continues to make an exception for the postal worker. He seems to enjoy barking when the post arrives, although he doesn't actually chew it up. The postal worker is obviously intimidated, though – he's started to prop your parcels against the door, rather than ringing the bell.

If it's just the postal worker that attracts your dog's attention in this way, you need the two to meet and make friends. Once your dog has officially 'met' him, he's unlikely to raise the same level of excitement. Most postal workers will be happy to go along with this provided you're only asking for a minute of their time. Ask your postal worker to knock on a specific day (you want to be in control of the situation when he does). Leave an open packet of your dog's favourite treats outside.

1 When the postal worker knocks, be ready with your dog on a lead inside. Open the door, lead him outside and ask the postal worker to throw treats to him from a few paces away.

2   When your dog moves towards him or her, 'introduce' them and have the worker feed the dog a couple of treats directly.

DOG'S-EYE VIEW

GETTING RESULTS

People wonder why I'm so keen on barking ferociously when the post person arrives. One of the reasons I like it is because they're one of the people who always, always respects my bark and goes away promptly. Job done. Sometimes my in-house person tells me off for doing it, but often they're off elsewhere in the house doing something else, and I have free rein to bark as much as I like. Sometime I grab a corner of the mail as it comes through the door and worry it fiercely for added effect. Recently, though, my owner's begun introducing me properly. There are treats involved, too.

3   From this point, ask your postal worker to post another couple of treats through the door along with the post. Now they've met, your dog's intensity towards him or her is likely to be reduced, and treats should seal the deal.

115

SHOULD WE TRY
CRATE TRAINING?

There are different opinions on this one, mostly because the use of crates is so often abused. Often the reason a dog doesn't like his crate is because his associations with it aren't good. Crate training has to be done carefully, so that the dog associates it with positive things – toys, food, comfort – before the door is ever closed. If only perfunctory efforts are made to give him a treat in his crate, and then the door is shut and he is left in it for some time, he can quickly come to associate it with loneliness and frustration, not pleasant downtime.

1 Originally crates were used as house-training aids for puppies (who don't like soiling where they sleep, so will try to avoid weeing while in a crate) and as 'safe places' for puppies and dogs when their owners couldn't keep an eye on them.

2 While crates can work well for both these things – and plenty of dogs who have been carefully crate-trained opt to spend time in their crate even when the door is open and they're free to go elsewhere – dogs are often left for far too long shut up in them. Also, since a puppy under six or seven months doesn't have reliable bladder control, he'll inevitably soil his crate if left in it for long, which can upset the whole house-training process.

DOG'S-EYE VIEW

TIME TO SETTLE

Although I'm not enthusiastic about being left, I've felt safer since they put me in my crate when they go out for an hour or so. I think they thought that I'd prefer to have free run of the house, but I find it actually makes me more nervous, as though I have to look after the whole place. And there's a dog opposite that barks a lot, and if I can get to the window, I feel I have to look out and bark back. I know that not all dogs feel the same way: some of my canine friends just go to sleep on the furniture as soon as their people go out, but I'm not like that, and I'm glad that they've realized that, in this situation, I'm the dog who prefers reassurance rather than space to range in.

3 Do you need your dog to like his crate? Since his associations with it already aren't good, rather than trying to retrain him to give him a positive view of it, it may be easier and less stressful all round if you put a comfortable bed for him in the kitchen, with a child gate in the doorway, so he's confined to a part of the house, but not shut up.

HOW TO DISTRACT FROM
HUMPING

Be honest: what owners most mind when their dog humps in public is the embarrassment factor – especially if the dog opts for a human leg rather than a soft toy or a cushion. So there are two parts to the problem: the humping dog and the red-faced owner.

WHY DO DOGS DO IT?

Humping is common to males and females, neutered and intact dogs, puppies and seniors: it's natural dog behaviour. Experts believe that it doesn't necessarily have much to do with sex and nor – even when done by one dog to another in a non-mating context – does it indicate a desire to 'dominate'. It's likely that some dogs use mounting as a stress reliever – to an overexcited dog, it may be an accessible way to calm himself down. Unless he does it obsessively, humping his pillow may well be the canine equivalent of a stress-relieving half-hour at the gym.

1

First ask yourself if it actually needs to stop. You may not want to watch, but if it's an occasional activity that he seems to use to help calm himself down, then the easiest route is to put his preferred toy or cushion in another room where he can find it if he wants to. If the object of his affection is another dog, or a human leg, that's a little more difficult.

WHEN TO SEEK HELP

There's a difference, though, between occasional humping and a dog who constantly mounts in an obsessive way. Very occasionally, humping becomes a compulsive behaviour that the dog can't stop. If humping turns into a routine during which he seems to get exhausted and distressed, but refuses to stop for even the most alluring distraction, something else is going on and you may need professional input to help change the pattern.

Don't ever punish your dog for humping, or grab his collar to pull him away; instead, call or lure him away from the other dog, or ask the leg's owner to remove it from range as efficiently as possible while you try distraction tactics. A squeaky toy heard from another room, the fridge door opening or even the doorbell ringing are all possibilities for getting his attention without a huge amount of fuss.

When he comes away, too, give him a treat; you're not rewarding him for humping, but for coming when he's asked.

119

TAKING THE STRESS OUT OF MEETING
NEW PEOPLE

When strangers make a dog anxious, it's usually because he's afraid. Maybe he wasn't socialized widely enough as a puppy, or maybe he hasn't been in enough different situations or met a wide enough range of people as an adult. If he's naturally slightly shy or nervous, that may aggravate the problem. Whatever the initial reason he began to find strangers intimidating, he's started either to weave behind you at the approach of someone he doesn't know, or, worse, to stand by you growling.

1 He can learn that good things happen around strangers. Since the fear is fairly non-specific (unlike dogs who are scared of people wearing sunglasses, say, or of tall men in hats), all you need are a number of strangers and a handful of his favourite treats. If you're not easily embarrassed, you can take a fast-talking friend and your dog to a busy nearby street and walk off to one side, while your friend walks 20 metres (65 feet) ahead of you handing out treats to everyone he or she meets to toss towards your dog as they approach him. (Your friend will need to stress that they shouldn't try to reach towards the dog or hand him the treat, just throw it in his direction as they walk by.)

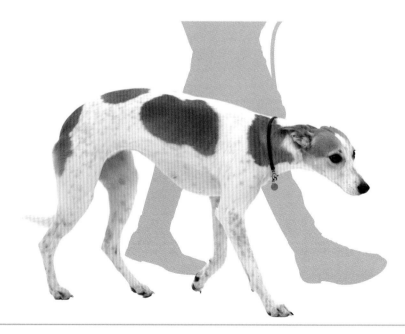

2 If the sidewalk solution feels a bit public to you, arrange to have people your dog doesn't know meet you in a park and practise in the same way. Any time he sees a stranger, he gets a treat. Keep the exercise short, but do it often, a couple of times daily if you can. It's a classic piece of counter-conditioning – strangers have become associated with pieces of chicken, which means that ultimately he'll feel anticipation rather than fear at the sight of them.

DOG'S-EYE VIEW

PASS ON BY

Recently, treats have begun to appear on the ground around me when people who I don't know pass by. It's helping to make me think differently about feeling afraid: after all, if random treats just appear in their vicinity, perhaps they're not all bad: it gives me more positive feelings towards them. And it's not as though they come up to me and hand treats over (that always made me very afraid when I didn't know them). Instead, they keep their distance. It's a win/win, and the bonus treats are helping me to relax.

WHEN TO GET
PROFESSIONAL HELP

Sometimes a problem with your dog reaches the point where you know that you and he aren't going to be able to resolve it alone. But when you decide that it's time to call in the professionals, where should you look? What's the difference between a trainer and a behaviourist and what sort of qualifications do they need. How can you find someone who will understand you, your dog and the problem, and use kind, positive methods to help?

WHAT THE TERMS MEAN

Trainers teach a dog to perform certain actions (or, in some cases, to stop performing them). They might, for example, help you to teach a strong dog to walk more easily on a lead.

Behaviourists look at the underlying reasons for a dog's behaviour – seeing the behaviour as a symptom rather than the cause – and at ways of modifying that behaviour by changing the way in which a dog feels about a situation. If an on-lead dog lunges and barks whenever he sees another dog, for example, they will look at finding ways to reduce his fear as a way of solving the problem. They treat a wide range of problems, including the most challenging, such as separation anxiety or fear-based aggression.

There are also trainer/behaviourists out there who combine the two roles. Finding the right person is made trickier by the fact that someone with no formal qualifications can still set up business as a dog trainer or a behaviourist without breaking the law. This means that some very old-fashioned practices linger on in the less regulated corners of the dog training-and-behaviour world, including punishment-based techniques that have long since been proved to be ineffective as well as inhumane.

However, the Animal Behaviour and Training Council (ABTC), a comparatively new regulatory body, has been working in the UK since 2009 to establish agreed standards for the knowledge and skills needed by trainers and behaviourists. Their recommendation for an Applied Animal Behaviourist is a minimum qualification of a BSc in Animal Behaviour, which means that ABTC behaviourists will have spent at least three years studying the subject.

The ABTC maintains national registers of qualified trainers and behaviourists (and their practitioner organizations, such as the Association of Pet Dog Trainers and The Canine Behaviour and Training Society), so when you're looking for the right person to help you, these will be a good place to start. Any reputable trainer or behaviourist who is practising now should focus exclusively on positive methods.

It should go without saying, but we'll say it anyway: no reputable practitioner will use physical force or coercion on a dog, nor 'aversives', such as shock collars or pads (not yet illegal in England, although they are now banned in Scotland and Wales, and in many other countries), nor anything that aims to scare the dog into obedience such as exaggerated yelling or jerked lead corrections.

WORKING WITH YOU

A good practitioner, whether trainer or behaviourist, will pay attention to you as well as to your dog. Think through any problems and concerns in detail before an appointment so that you can pinpoint and describe apparent triggers that set a behaviour off, the contexts in which it arises, how you behave when it does, and so on. Expect (and be ready to answer) plenty of questions about your behaviour as well as your dog's – this isn't intrusive, it's just fact-gathering. Be open-minded about what you hear: to help your pet to change his behaviour, you are likely to need to modify some things about your own.

FURTHER READING

BENDIX, KATE
Top Dog (London, 2014)
Full guide to keeping your dog well and healthy. Particularly good
on all the complicated detail of different diets for dogs and their
pros and cons.

BRADSHAW, JOHN
In Defence of Dogs (London, 2011)
The Animals Among Us (London, 2017)
In *In Defence of Dogs*, Bradshaw wrote one of the first appealing
and accessible mainstream books about how dogs have come to
live alongside humans and how they arrived at the companion
status they have today. *The Animals Among Us* broadens the
discussion and looks at contemporary life with companion animals.

CLOTHIER, SUZANNE
Bones Would Rain from the Sky (New York, 2005)
Recounting the experiences of a dog owner and behaviourist
dealing with all kinds of problems in all kinds of dogs.

COPPINGER, RAYMOND & FEINSTEIN, MARK
How Dogs Work (Chicago, 2015)
Academic but still readable study that does what it says: looks
at what is known about how dogs work, both physiologically
and mentally.

COREN, STANLEY
How to Speak Dog (New York, 2000)
One of the first books to look at the 'languages' dogs speak and
at how humans can begin to understand them.

HARE, BRIAN, AND WOODS, VANESSA
The Genius of Dogs (New York, 2013)
An in-depth study of the intelligence of dogs, and how scientists know what they know about how dogs think.

HOROWITZ, ALEXANDRA
Inside of a Dog (New York, 2009)
Being a Dog (New York, 2016)
Two beautifully written, scholarly and imaginative books that look at what we can deduce – from the state of current research – about the experience of being a dog. *Being a Dog*, in particular, offers fascinating insights into what it might be like to have a dog's scenting ability.

McCONNELL, PATRICIA
The Other End of the Leash (New York, 2002)
For the Love of a Dog (New York, 2007)
Tales of Two Species (Washington, 2009)
McConnell is one of the best-known and most highly regarded behaviourists and ethologists in the US today. All three books are full of stories of her personal experiences as a professional working with dogs and packed with information that any dog owner will find illuminating and helpful.

MIKLÓSI, ÁDÁM
Dog Behaviour, Evolution, and Cognition (Oxford, 2007)
A one-stop shop if you've ever been curious about canine cognition. It's a packed academic book that covers all aspects of a very big subject, and is also an engrossing read.

INDEX

A

ABTC (Animal Behaviour and Training Council) 123
accidents 44–5, 46, 47–9, 116
anxiety/stress 14, 32, 83, 87, 95, 104–5, 120–1, 122
aromatherapy 69
aversives 123

B

ball junkies 102–3
barking 12, 19, 42, 50, 51, 56, 67, 83, 104, 114, 115
beagles 13
begging 112
behavioural studies 7, 23, 29, 34, 36–7, 51, 98
behaviourists 122–3
bloodhounds 13, 31
body language 15, 24, 27, 28–33, 56, 82–3, 87, 88–90
bones 65, 103
bullying 28, 88–9

C

calming signals 29
caudate nucleus 27
charging at the door 50–3
chasing 59, 77, 78, 80, 86–7, 88–9
chewing 65, 103
children 18–19
citizens 7
cognition studies 7, 23, 24–5, 26–7, 34
collars 69, 73, 81, 123
collies 25

commercially produced food 62, 63, 64–5
communication 15, 24–5, 28–33
competitive games 22
confidence 15, 21, 33, 37, 49, 90, 95
consistency 18, 41, 43, 66, 112
cooperation 34, 35
Coren, Stanley 25
cortisol 83
crates 42, 47, 48, 98, 116–17
crowds 57

D

DAP (Dog Appeasing Pheromone) 69
deliberate communication 28
dens 43, 44
diet 62–5
digestibility 64–5
distractions 50, 73, 75, 78–9, 89, 94
dogwatching 21
dominance 36–7, 118
dopamine 103
drooling 104

E

ears 12, 31, 82
eating 19, 42, 47, 58, 62–5, 112–13
empathy 27
expectations 6, 24–7
exploring 42, 91
eyes 29, 30, 101

F

fear 18, 26, 30, 32, 33, 36, 37,

54–7, 82–5, 90–1, 92–5, 120–1, 122
feelings/emotions 26–7, 28
fetch 19, 20, 22, 58, 102–3
flexibility 99
front doors 38, 50–3, 93–5
furniture 98, 108–9

G

games 19, 20–1, 22–3, 47, 58, 59, 77, 79–80, 86–8, 111
German shepherds 13, 31
grief 106–7
growling 19, 56, 88, 100, 108, 110, 120
guarding 58, 61, 100–101
guilt 26, 27

H

hard eyes 30, 101
harnesses 73
hearing/listening 12, 18, 19, 82–5
heel, walking to 16, 75
high alert 14
home alone 104–5
home-cooked food 62, 63, 64
house-training 38, 42, 44–9, 116
howling 12, 104
hugging 17
humping 118–19
hunting 18, 35

I

illness 92
incontinence 49
instinct 15, 34
involuntary communication 28

J
jumping up 19, 66, 67, 69

K
knowledge 7, 20–3, 88

L
lateral thinking 93, 96
leads 16, 57, 72–5, 77, 81, 91, 95, 122, 123
learning 6, 25, 46, 98–9
licking 17
loneliness 15, 104–5, 116
looking 14, 18
loud noises 12, 18, 19, 82–5
love 27

M
marking 13, 42, 49
misconceptions 34, 35, 36, 37
mouths 32–3, 82
muzzles 91

N
natural behaviour 10, 12–15, 118
nipping 7, 19, 66, 67, 89, 91, 96, 110–11

O
observation 14, 15, 34
overexcitement 21, 50, 66–9, 82, 88–9, 102, 105, 118
oxytocin 27

P
pack animals 34, 35, 36
panting 104
pause time 66, 68–9, 88, 89
personality 20, 40, 41, 88, 90, 98, 107

play bows 28, 29, 87
play-fighting 32
play styles 20, 86, 87, 88
playing 19, 20–1, 22–3, 28, 29, 47, 58, 59, 66–8, 77, 79–80, 86–90, 102–3, 111
possessiveness 58–61, 96
postal workers 114–15
praising 42, 46, 47, 75, 80, 89
problem solving 98–9
professional help 104, 119, 122–3
pugs 13, 31
pulling (on the lead) 72–3
punishment 36, 119, 122
puppies 15, 40, 44, 46, 47, 48, 54, 69, 83, 107, 110, 116

R
raw food 62, 63, 64, 65, 103
recall 76–81, 89
roles 6, 35, 38, 86
routines 14, 41, 42, 94, 101, 105
Rugaas, Turid 29
rule of threes 40, 41

S
safety rules 19
scent 13, 27, 51, 54, 69, 78
separation anxiety 14, 95, 104, 122
settling 40–3, 49, 117
shyness 17, 21, 26, 28, 43, 90–1, 120
side-by-side walking 16, 74, 75
signs and signals 28–9, 44, 47, 82, 88, 89, 104–5
sits 19, 50, 52, 68–9, 81, 108–9
sleeping 19, 42, 47, 48, 116, 117
sniffing/smelling 13, 19, 27, 29, 42, 46, 47, 51, 54, 78, 91

social walks 90–1
socialization 15, 54, 86, 90, 91, 120
squinty eyes 29, 30
stays 50, 52–3
strangers 17, 54–7, 120–1
swap 58, 60–1

T
tails 27, 28, 32–3, 82, 89
taking turns 86, 87, 88
time out 66, 88, 89
tongue flick 29, 33
touching/handling 17, 18, 19, 27, 43, 56
toy fixation 100–103
toys 20, 22, 23, 60–1, 66–8, 79, 94, 95, 96, 100–103, 111
trainers 122–3
treats 19, 21, 34, 46–7, 52, 56–7, 60–1, 68–9, 73–5, 78–80, 83, 95, 100–101, 108–9, 114–15, 120–1
trick training 21, 103, 107
tucked tails 27, 28, 33, 82, 89
tug 20, 22–3, 111

U
uncertainty 31, 33, 37, 43
unnatural behaviour 16–19

W
walks 16, 25, 72-5, 90–5, 107, 122
weaving (on the lead) 72, 120
wheel of house-training 48
whining 47
wolves 34, 35, 36
wrestling 21, 77, 86–7, 88–9

Y
yawning 29

ACKNOWLEDGMENTS

With thanks to all the dogs and their owners:

Roo and Ellie
Snoop and Tanya
Edison and Veronika
Snoopy, Bear, Dave and Kara
Phoebe and Laura
Clarence and David
Agatha and Rowan
Freddie and Joe
Dizzy and Mark
Frankie and Chris
Ruby, Luna, Smudge and Tabitha
Ozzy and Soraya
Henry and Ailish
Hunny and Jennifer
Buddy and Ben

How was the book?
Please post your
feedback and photos:
#DogsEyeView

AMMONITE
PRESS

www.ammonitepress.com